# BREAD

*Books by* JOAN WIENER

Victory Through Vegetables
Get Your Health Together
The Illustrated Hassle-Free
    Make Your Own Clothes Book
Son of Hassle-Free Sewing

# BREAD

*Joan Wiener and Diana Collier*

J. B. LIPPINCOTT COMPANY
Philadelphia and New York

U.S. Library of Congress Cataloging in Publication Data

Wiener, Sita.
  Bread.

  1. Bread.   I. Collier, Diana, birth date    joint
author.   II. Title.
TX769.W53      641.8′15      73–1803
ISBN–0–397–00961–5

*Diana would like to thank her testers,
contributors, and helpers:
Raj and Madeline, Hank, Carol, Aidan, T. Finn,
Kirsten, Mrs. Mann, Alice, Tommy, Alex,
Mother, Oscar, Peg, Dora and Lizzy, Ruth,
Catherine, Hosea and Lois, Sophia, and Timmie,
a cairn terrier who liked our failures
as well as our successes.*

*Joan would like to thank her testers:
Shanti Daisy Doe, Richie, Sharon, Patty,
Doreen, Larry, Sean, Jeremy; and Shanku,
for her Indian recipes.*

# Contents

## YEAST BREADS

# BREAD

# Bread Power

Bread is as familiar to man as life itself, for it has preserved and sustained his existence for thousands and thousands of years—feeding him and nourishing his children and his children's children, giving him the strength to work out his destiny.

And for centuries, those who would control everybody else's body, mind, and emotions did so by controlling bread production—laying down dietary rules, setting up prices, restricting baking.

A hundred years after Christ's birth, Greek slaves formed the first bakers' union and produced different qualities of bread for the different classes—senator's bread, plebeian's bread, slave's bread. Around 1155, under King Henry II, two bread guilds were established—a White Bakers' and a Brown Bakers' Guild. Fine white bread was a status symbol reserved for the highborn and wealthy. In Scotland, the finest-textured white bread, "manchet," was baked for royalty and the great landowners; "cheat" was made for upper-class tradesmen; "raveled" (of whole grain flour) was bread for the middle-class villagers; and "mashloch" (coarse bran mixed with rye) fed the poor and the servant class. Eventually, laws were passed requiring bakers to add wheat germ to mashloch in order to improve the health of the lower classes.

In Paris the bakery business was controlled by the monks, who decreed no baking on Sundays and fete days. The proceeds of an oven tax went toward support and burial of the poor.

The lower-class British weren't allowed to have ovens at home but were forced to buy yeast at the bakery, prepare the bread at home, and bring it back to the bakery for cooking (where they might or might not get back their own loaves).

The pressures are still with us. Today big corporations—nonpersons—keep pushing their product—a spongy, squooshy, ghastly white, dehumanized, denutritized, preservatized, flavorized, propionated, artificialized, shot-up, brought-down item more closely related to a Styrofoam cup than the staff of life.

But the power to make your own bread is as simple and uncomplicated to regain as a trip to the health food store. There is no mystique to bread baking. Once you get into a sack of fresh, natural flour and some water, once you get over the old programmed admonishments about getting yourself messy and get down to the relationship between yourself and dough, a very basic, very cellular awareness seems to come up—as if you'd always, always been baking bread.

And you have, for all those thousands and thousands of years. You are simply bringing the bread power back home. It's your bread, not theirs.

# What Is Bread?

If we are really aware of what bread is, what makes it up, what conditions affect it, how we influence it, it becomes an old friend, no longer awesome or secret but nice to have around and easy to deal with. That doesn't eliminate the element of magic in bread making; it just means we are the magicians.

If you are no novice and you bake bread about as easily as you breathe, you probably know most of the information contained in these chapters preceding the recipes. You might skim them to see. Then move to the recipes.

And if you are new to bread making but eager to get down on some dough, you can manage with a quick reading of this section to see what's here—and then come back to find the information you need when you need it.

All bread is made by mixing flour or meal with some type of liquid. Usually a leavening is added, along with other ingredients for flavor and nutrition. The reason for this section is not merely to list but also to describe the many possible components that make up bread—just so you'll know what to shop for, what to expect of it, and how to handle it when you get into the kitchen.

## FLOUR AND MEAL

After a great deal of experimentation, decisions, and palatal and digestive judgments, we suggest that you use whole wheat flour, unbleached white flour (made from the endosperm of wheat—to be explained), rye flour and rye meal, cornmeal, oatmeal and oat flour, buckwheat flour, soy flour, and rice flour. Whole grains are available in health food stores and can be coarsely ground in a blender.

### Wheat Flour

Whole wheat and white flour both come from the wheat plant. Bran and wheat germ are also milled from the kernel or

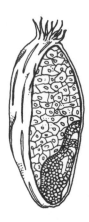

grain of the plant. Bran is the outer layer of the wheat kernel and makes up about 14 percent of the kernel's weight. Inside is the germ, which makes up about 3 percent. The remaining 83 percent is endosperm, food storage tissue and the source of white flour. The kernel is a composite of much starch, some protein, oil, cellulose fiber, minerals like calcium and iron, vitamin B complex, and vitamin E.

The difference between whole wheat and white flour is that the former uses all three parts of the kernel—bran, germ, and endosperm—while white just uses the endosperm; thus whole wheat breads are heavier, coarser, and more nutritious than white breads but take a longer time rising.

Stone-ground whole wheat flour is nicest. In the earliest mills, the whole wheat kernel was pounded between two stones until it was reduced to a powder. Later, millers developed the stone ground process used today a stationary millstone on the bottom, wheat fed in through a hopper, to be ground by an upper stone, turning fairly slowly. The power turning these stones can be people, mules, horses, oxen, windmills, water-wheels, dynamos. Stone grinding preserves the nutritive value of the wheat because the wheat remains relatively cool during milling.

White bread is the offspring of greed and "appearance for appearance's sake." It began with the discovery that flour could be stored longer without spoiling if the wheat germ was removed. Next they separated coarse, dark bran from the white endosperm because white was beautiful, indicative of purity, virginity, cleanliness. In eighteenth-century England so many additives had been put in bread to obtain these results that a campaign was begun to abolish alum, marble dust, carbonate of lead, and other chemicals from bread as they were ruining the health of "the entire population of London."

Eventually the commercial bakers concluded that when flour was aged its baking quality improved. Instead of allowing even this process to occur naturally, science discovered that chemical bleaching sped up the aging process. The color of white flour now changed from a creamy color to chalky white—even better! Today in flour mills high-speed rollers crack the wheat kernels, separating the germ, bran, and endosperm—sifting away the germ and bran to be sold as livestock feed—removing most of the vitamins and minerals. Some states require millers to pump synthetic nutrients back into their white flour, but if you want to bake your own white bread, we suggest adding yeast, honey, molasses, soy flour, wheat germ, malt, brewer's yeast, and milk.

While we specify *unbleached white* in our white flour recipes, you can make the breads with *all-purpose flour*, which you can get everywhere. However, the unbleached white is popping up more frequently as the demand increases—and it's worth looking for. If you can't find it locally, you can order it by mail from one of the "Sources of Basic Equipment and Ingredients" listed at the end of this book.

Wheat Germ

In many of our recipes we use wheat germ as an ingredient because of its taste and high nutritive value. You can find it in most supermarkets in the form of toasted wheat germ and in health food stores as raw wheat germ. Regardless of where you buy your wheat germ, carefully read the label to make sure it has no additives. We prefer the purity of raw wheat germ.

After opening the container of either kind, keep it in the refrigerator so that it will not turn rancid.

## Bran

This part of wheat, the outer coating of the wheat kernel, is available in most health food stores as pure bran, bran flakes, bran, etc. Don't confuse this product with "All-Bran" breakfast cereal available in supermarkets because "All-Bran" will not work in our recipes.

## Graham Flour

This is whole wheat flour but with the bran left coarse and flaky instead of being ground slowly to a consistently fine powder. When a recipe calls for graham flour, you may substitute whole wheat flour.

## Whole Wheat Pastry Flour

This is a particularly finely ground whole soft-wheat flour usually used in pastries. It's available in health food stores.

While wheat flour is the most commonly used, interesting breads can be made from many other grains:

## Rye Flour and Meal

This is a darker grain which is ground fine for flour, coarser for meal. Joan's friend Frenchie tells us, flexing his biceps, that rye builds muscle while wheat builds fat and he tossed all the chub-producing wheat flour out of his cupboard, but we don't really know much about that. Rye, like wheat flour, does contain gluten (see "Gluten," below) and can be used alone or with wheat flour or cornmeal.

Oats

A grain most people recognize as rolled oats or oatmeal, oats are associated in childhood memory banks with breakfast—yummy and nourishing, or an unfortunate pasty-gray assemblage of blaaaa/yecch. Rolled oats are produced by softening the grain with water and rolling to flatten. Oats also come steel-cut into flakes or ground into a light-grayish-brownish flour that combines nicely with wheat and rye.

Buckwheat

Buckwheat can be ground into a coarse, light-brown flour flecked with black particles. It's applauded in pancakes, waffles, and bread, and can stand alone or be used with wheat flour, rye flour, or cornmeal. It is also eaten as buckwheat groats or kasha. It took Joan a long time to realize that buckwheat was really kasha using an assumed name. She used to eat it cooked with water and added to bowtie noodles under the heading *kasha varnischkas.*

Corn

A native American grain which may be ground to medium meal or to flour consistency. Both the yellow corn and white corn varieties of cornmeal are frequently used in bread, though yellow contains more nutrients. Make sure to get "whole grain" cornmeal rather than "degerminated," as the corn germ (like the wheat germ) is a vital part of the grain. Cornmeal is also used in conjunction with wheat, rye, or other flours. We also use cornmeal in loaf pans and on baking sheets to prevent bread from sticking and to add to the flavor.

Corn flour is available either white or yellow and is whole ground to a fine consistency (more so than cornmeal). It can be used in combination with whole wheat flour, rye, white flour, or wheat germ and is nice in our American Indian Bread recipe.

Soy Flour

Modern man suffers from "protein paranoia"—the fear of not getting enough protein in his daily regimen. To counteract this affliction, soy dosage is recommended as soybeans are a high-protein food. In fact, if you want to increase the protein content of your bread (can't hurt), add a small amount of soy flour (or soy powder, available in health food stores) in place of an equal amount of the recipe's main flour. If you want to eliminate soy flour from a recipe (as in cases of P. OD.— protein overdose), make up the difference with the recipe's main flour.

Rice Flour

Both unpolished or brown rice and polished or white rice (God forbid, intone our macrobiotic friends) can be ground into flour and used in bread recipes. White rice is mainly starch, though, while brown rice retains many of the vitamins and nutriments. When used in large quantities, rice flour has a pastry-like texture and can be substituted in hot-cake and waffle recipes.

Gluten

Something different from glutton, which is a possible by-product of gluten. It is a protein contained in the endosperm of the wheat and the heaviest part of the flour. When flour is mixed with water and then kneaded, gluten absorbs the water, expanding to form microscopic strands which spread through the mixture and provide the toughness, strength, and elasticity of both wheat flour dough and (to a lesser extent) rye dough. In many wheat flour recipes, you'll see an instruction like "Knead well to develop gluten" or "Knead until dough is smooth, elastic, and springy." When yeast is added to the dough, it produces carbon dioxide gas, which causes the dough to rise. Then gluten provides the strength for the dough to hold its risen shape. That's why glutenless cornmeal, soy, and rice doughs don't rise so well with most of their yeast gas frittering away.

Some people react badly to gluten, developing iliac disease. This disease can be cured simply enough by avoiding wheat and rye flours.

## Potato Flour

This is milled from whole potatoes, cooked and dried. It takes 5 pounds potatoes to make 1 pound potato flour, which is best used in combination with other flours in breads, pancakes, muffins, etc. When adding it to recipes, blend it with other flours before adding liquids, to prevent lumping.


# LIQUIDS

## Water

The proper water temperature is crucial to bread baking. Various recipes call for anything from boiling hot to ice water.

Use boiling water to soften oatmeal, cornmeal, certain groats, and farina, as well as to sterilize mixtures like home yeast culture medium and the containers for sponges, sourdoughs, and sour preparations.

With yeast breads, body temperature water should be used to soften, separate, and activate the yeast cells. Test the temperature by sprinkling some water inside your wrist. When it's neither hot nor cold, it's just right. As water approaches freezing, yeast cells become inactive. If water is too hot to touch, it will kill them. Their favorite climate is somewhere between 70°–115°.

Cold water is useful in preparing certain unleavened breads —particularly crackers or wafers—and for glazing bread. Needless to say, your water should always be clean, wholesome, and sanitary. When in doubt, boil it to discourage the growth of any unwelcome bacteria which can affect the taste, flavor, and aroma of your bread.

---

Milk

Recipes in this book call for whole milk (your everyday pasteurized, homogenized milk-next-store), skim milk, milk diluted with water, buttermilk, and nonfat dry milk. (*Note:* Nonfat dry milk is most often used in powder form here.)

A way to double the amount of milk protein in a bread without increasing your amount of dough is to use the amount of dry milk powder called for to make 1 quart, but mix it with only 1 pint of liquid.

If a recipe didn't rise well, next time substitute skim milk or a mixture of nonfat dry milk for whole milk. Sometimes the fat content in the latter inhibits rising. Dry milk is also cheaper, easier to handle, can be stored, and has less acidity and sugar content than whole milk. White breads made with dry milk brown evenly, have more tender crusts, and their crumbs stay softer longer than those produced by whole milk.

In yeast bread recipes, you're directed to scald the milk. This is because the rising time necessary in yeast breads causes whole milk to stand at room temperature for an hour or more, and there's a possibility that the milk may sour even though already mixed into the dough. Scalding the milk before using it in a recipe slows down the souring process. While buttermilk in breads can taste outofsight, partly soured sweet milk is yicky.

To scald milk, put it in a pan over low heat until it begins to boil. Then take off heat and stir. Be sure to cool the milk to 100° or body temperature before using in yeast bread.

In biscuit and muffin baking scalding is not necessary, as these products are placed in the oven immediately so souring can't occur.

Eggs

While eggs add protein, minerals, vitamins, rising ability, and cohesiveness to bread, they also add considerably to the liquid content (1 medium egg = 2 ounces). This means it may be necessary to juggle your bread's flour content—increasing or decreasing flour—when halving or doubling recipes. In this book, we've interchangeably used "Large Grade A" and "Medium Grade A" eggs, which are actually not very different in size.

Be precise in egg treatment. If a recipe calls for "slightly beaten eggs" 10–15 strokes with a fork will do better than whipping vigorously with a rotary beater. For "well-beaten eggs" whale away with aforementioned beater, wire whisk, or 50–up strokes with a fork to create something light and homogenized.

When a recipe calls for separating the yolk from the white, do so into 2 dry containers. It is more important to keep the yolk away from the white than the white away from the yolk.

Don't expect much lightness from beating yolks—they are fairly heavy and oily. When you beat whites, make sure to begin with a clean, dry beater and bowl. The tiniest speck of water, yolk, batter, or other extraneous material can keep whites from becoming light, foamy, and stiff.

Eggs are also used in glazing breads.

Potato Water

This is the water saved after the boiled potatoes have been removed. Use it instead of plain water for its nice potato flavor and because its starch content feeds the yeast and aids rising. Bear in mind that it produces a coarser bread than the breads made with other liquids.

Other Liquids

Other liquids, used for Glazing and as Flavorings, will be described under those headings.


LEAVENING

Breads are leavened by air, water vapor (steam), and gases (usually carbon dioxide). Leavening agents such as yeast and baking powder, when activated, produce gas bubbles within the dough, and the process is helped along by the action of air and steam.

Even unleavened breads like crackers and wafers are leavened to some extent during baking by the expansion of air trapped in the dough or batter, and of steam; or by the action of wild yeasts and bacteria from the air, growing in the dough and releasing gases.

## Air

Air is introduced into bread by almost all the ways you handle the flour in the various stages of bread making—sifting, stirring, mixing, beating, and lifting the flour with the fingertips. Beaten egg whites trap a great many air bubbles which, when they are folded into a batter, provide lightness as well as space in which steam can expand to raise the bread even further. The dough of certain non-yeast breads must be beaten or folded over many times for leavening to occur.

## Steam

Steam plays a part in the raising of all breads, but one of the most visible illustrations of this process is in popovers. When the thin, well-beaten batter of flour, eggs, and milk is put into cups and then into a hot oven, it produces large hollow shells.

## Yeast

Yeast is a microscopic living plant. When put in dough or batter containing starch or sugar and kept at a temperature somewhere between 40°–115°, it grows and multiplies, producing carbon dioxide gas. These gas bubbles aid in raising the bread and making it light.

*Active dry yeast* seems to work best for us (it's also called *package yeast*—or, in our recipes, simply *dry yeast*) and comes in 1-pound or ½-pound packages, individual 1-tablespoon packages (a good buy if you only bake once in a while) or in unlimited quantity, loose, at certain health food stores—but here there is the problem of whether or not it is fresh. And yeast should be fresh for best results. After a package is opened, store your unused yeast in a tight container in a cool, dry place like your refrigerator.

Further on, you'll find recipes for making your own yeast and "starters" for sourdough breads. Making your own yeast at home is not difficult, as yeast spores are widely present in the air. However, results are not always as uniform as when you use commercial yeast in your bread.

As for *sourdough*, that's a yeast culture made by preserving some uncooked dough that's been allowed to rise at a moderately low temperature (like your refrigerator). Remembering that this yeast culture is alive, you must feed it a little flour or sugar and water from time to time to sustain it and help it multiply.

When mixing up your bread recipe, put 1 tablespoon or more of dry yeast into ¼–½ cup of body-temperature water, stir, let stand a few minutes until slightly bubbly, and then finally mix with the other ingredients. Often, the other liquids in the recipe are warmed first to encourage rapid growth of the yeast. However, if these liquids are too hot (if your hand isn't comfortable in them), they may kill off the yeast plants and the bread will not rise properly.

The temperature for the rising of yeast breads should be somewhere between 70° and 85°. We found 70°–80° to be best, for even though this isn't the fastest rising temperature for bread, it creates an even, fine-textured bread. At temperatures higher than the range of 70°–85°, bread may rise unevenly and develop an off-taste because bacteria will grow along with the yeast.

To speed up the rising process by as much as 1 hour, you can add 1 additional package or tablespoon of yeast. If you avoid high temperatures, this extra yeast won't create a funky, yeasty taste.

For finest bread texture, put your dough in the refrigerator overnight for one of its risings. The cool temperature will slow down the rising, but not stop it completely. This is not recommended for yeast-rising batter breads.

Some brands of package yeast are dated to tell you how long the yeast will continue to be usable, but if you have any doubts about the yeast's vitality, test it in the following manner. Sprinkle 1 teaspoon yeast into ¼ cup body-temperature water along with ½ teaspoon sugar and ½ teaspoon flour. Cover and set in a warm place for 10–15 minutes. If it has doubled and is foaming, you know it's safe to use. It is disappointing to go through a complete dough-making process, only to have your mixture fail to rise.

*Doubling or halving recipes.* If you wish to double a recipe it is not necessary to increase the yeast more than 1½ times. If the recipe suggests 2 Tbsp or 2 pkgs yeast, use only 3 Tbsp or 3 pkgs. And remember, the rising time will be longer.

If you wish to halve a recipe take ½ of each ingredient. However, if the original recipe calls for only 1 Tbsp or 1 pkg yeast, do not halve the yeast—use the full amount.

You can, if you like, make your own yeast cakes. Their addition to rye breads makes a subtle change in texture and flavor. Here is a recipe:

## HOMEMADE YEAST CAKES

| | |
|---|---|
| 1½ | cups buttermilk |
| ¼ | tsp salt |
| 5 | cups cornmeal (3 cups to be sterilized) |
| 1 | Tbsp or 1 pkg dry yeast |
| ¼ | cup water, body temperature |
| 1½ | cups or more unsifted unbleached white flour |

In good-size glass or unchipped enamel saucepan stir together 1½ cups buttermilk, ¼ tsp salt, and 2 cups cornmeal. Heat to boiling, lower heat, and cook 5 minutes, stirring constantly to prevent burning. Cool to body temperature.

In cup stir 1 Tbsp or pkg dry yeast into ¼ cup water, body temperature. Stir into cornmeal-buttermilk mixture, cover with a cloth, and leave in warm place (about 75°–85°) until it rises and becomes fluffy, which might take several hours (it won't quite double in bulk). Stir, and let rise again until light—do this 4 or 5 times.

In large shallow pan, toast slightly (to sterilize) remaining 3 cups cornmeal in 350° oven, stirring it several times to keep it from burning. Let cornmeal cool. Mix 1½ cups toasted cornmeal with 1½ cups unsifted unbleached white flour, leaving remainder in pan.

Stir flour-cornmeal mixture into yeast mixture until you have a stiff dough which comes away from sides of pan, adding more flour if necessary. Turn out onto clean board and knead several times. Roll out to ½-inch thickness. Cut into 1-inch to 1½-inch squares with sharp knife.

Lift up squares with spatula and place them on top of remaining cornmeal in flat pan, turning them over to coat both sides with dry toasted cornmeal. Set pan in dry place at room temperature, turning cakes from time to time, until dry (3 or 4 days).

To store, line can or jar with paper towels and stack yeast cakes with paper towels between. Close tightly and keep in refrigerator.

To use, crumble cakes with fingers or grate as fine as possible. Use 1 cake in place of 1 Tbsp or pkg of dry yeast. Action will be slower than commercial yeast.


Baking Powder

Baking powder is a mixture of bicarbonate of soda (baking soda) with an acid and some cornstarch or flour which serves to keep the soda (a base) and acid apart until the baking powder is dissolved in liquid. When the soda and acid finally do come together they react, forming a salt and carbon dioxide gas. It is these gas bubbles which cause the bread to rise.

Baking powder comes "single acting" or "double acting," but the two can be used interchangeably in our recipes. Double-acting baking powder is a combination of single-acting baking powder plus sodium aluminum sulfate, or is a mixture of cornstarch, bicarbonate of soda, sodium aluminum phosphate, and other materials. Because of the additives many people prefer using single-acting baking powder.

Commercial baking powder is satisfactory, or you can make it yourself. Count on using 1½ tsp baking powder for each cup of flour in the recipes that use this rising method.

Here is a recipe for one kind of single-acting baking powder:

1 part cornstarch
2 parts bicarbonate of soda
4 parts cream of tartar

Sift the 3 ingredients together several times and it is ready for use. Cream of tartar, created by the fermentation of grapes in wine making, is the necessary acid material. (It works too as a method for removing burn stains from pots—something we learned from Joan's mother.)

## Baking Soda

Baking soda is used as a leavening agent in certain of our breads. It reacts with an acid ingredient—such as buttermilk, sour cream, fruit—to produce carbon dioxide gas, which raises the bread. The usual proportions are: approximately ½ tsp soda to 1 cup buttermilk or sour cream in recipes such as Sour Cream Biscuits, Rich Irish Bread, Buttermilk Waffles.

When you make breads with either baking soda or baking

powder, mix the batter or dough quickly and get it into a pre-heated oven. The rising action takes place very fast and the bread may fall if it's not rapidly baked and set.

## FLAVORINGS

### Salt

The most frequently used flavoring in bread is salt. Baking powder and baking soda breads usually take 1 tsp salt per 2 cups flour; yeast breads, 1 tsp per 3 cups flour, added to the dry ingredients rather than to the yeast mixture. Too much salt can inhibit yeast action.

Salt water used to glaze French and Italian breads gives them their tempting light brown crusts. Coarse salt adds flavor and decoration to the surface of bread and rolls.

When we mention butter in our recipes, we mean the sweet, unsalted variety, but if you do use salted butter, reduce slightly the amount of salt in the recipe.

### Sugar

Bad-mouthing on the part of health food *mavens* is creating a generation of "sugophobics"—those who avoid sugar like bubonic plague. Undaunted, we're thoroughly hooked and continue to use it. Though light brown sugar differs from the white variety only because of the addition of some molasses, we prefer its folksy taste and the rustic warm color it gives bread crusts. Brown sugar keeps better if placed in an airtight container like a jar or can or sealed plastic bag. Our friend Sharon insists that putting a vanilla bean in the sugar bowl keeps the sugar from drying out and gives it a lush vanilla scent. Diana holds with the technique of adding a whole apple to rock-hard sugar in order to soften it again.

Always break up lumps in your sugar before using it in

bread. Always measure brown sugar firmly packed. Unless it conflicts with your recipe, dissolve sugar in liquids rather than mixing with the dry ingredients.

In any recipe, white or dark brown sugar can be substituted for the light brown kind we like. Dark brown will change the color of the loaf.

Honey

Diana definitely prefers natural, unheated honey to the less expensive (usually) heated variety. Joan can't tell the difference between unheated and heated, but there are obvious differences in honeys coming from different plants and locations —ranging from light and bland to dark and potent. It's interesting to try a number of them. If you use a lot of honey, it's more economical to buy it in 5-pound containers.

In most recipes you can substitute honey for sugar, but be sure to add a little more. Keep in mind that honey has a stronger flavor than sugar; also that you might have to put in a little more flour because honey will add liquid to your mixture.

Molasses

Molasses is used as a sweetener, in place of sugar, and also to flavor and color dark breads. Blackstrap and crude molasses make your bread darker than the other kinds.

In the recipe testing, we tried regular unsulphured molasses, blackstrap, crude, Jamaican, Barbados, and sorghum, which were all good, though different from one another.

While molasses is the boiled and condensed juice of the sugar cane, sorghum is the boiled and condensed juice of the sorghum stalk. The latter can be substituted for molasses and makes for a refreshing change of flavor.

Malt Syrup

This syrup, made from barley, can be used in place of dark

brown molasses to add color and a slightly bitter flavor (quite nice) to breads like rye bread. Malt syrup works best when melted into a warm liquid ingredient of a recipe. It tends to slow down the rising of yeast breads. After you open a can of malt syrup, store it in the refrigerator; before using, put the can in a pan of warm water for a few minutes to liquefy it.

## Unsweetened Chocolate

Unsweetened chocolate is used in some recipes for both its flavor and its dark, rich color. Melt it slowly to avoid burning (some say burned chocolate is poisonous), and mix it with some or all of the liquid ingredients.

One square weighs 1 ounce.

## Coffee

When employed for bread baking, coffee can be a freshly brewed liquid, or used in powdered or freeze-dried instant form. You add it more for color than flavor, though the taste combines nicely with things like chocolate and molasses in dark breads. It can also be used as a glaze.

## Beer

A good thing to use as a substitute for water when making rye bread. We use ordinary local stuff, but you can experiment with ale, stout, dark beer, imported beer, homebrew. Use beer at room temperatures in bread making. During baking, most of the alcohol evaporates.

## Sourdough

Sourdough, the dough saved from a previous mixing and raising of yeast-rising bread, is permeated with yeast and has a sour smell. You can use it effectively instead of active dry yeast, though your bread will rise more slowly, or you can add it to active dry to create a distinctive, stimulating flavor. Always keep it in a closed container only partially filled, in your refrigerator or any other cool, dry place. Sourdoughphiles keep a supply constantly on hand by saving a cup or two of risen dough from each batch of bread.

Brewer's Yeast

Here we mean the by-product yeast left after brewing rather than the active yeast used in brewing beer. Never substitute brewer's yeast for active dry in these recipes, as it will not start the fermentation and rising of bread. Mainly, we use it for its flavor and to increase the protein content. It's almost 50 percent protein and has such a distinctive (some would say "disgusting") flavor, we suggest you use it with a deft hand—say no more than 1 Tbsp to a loaf of bread. Even if a recipe calls for more, you can reduce the amount or leave it out entirely as you like.

Seeds

A variety of small seeds are called for in our recipes. Some —like caraway, fennel, and anise—are put in for their pungent, aromatic flavor. Others—pumpkin, poppy, sunflower, and sesame seeds—have a pleasing texture. Both add to the visual appeal when used on the outside of breads. (An egg glaze will make them adhere.)

When using seeds in your dough, mix them first with some flour so they won't pop out as you knead. For a more intense flavor, crush them with a mortar and pestle.

Spices

Our recipes call for ground cinnamon, ground and crystallized ginger, ground mace, ground nutmeg, ground coriander, ground or crushed cardamom, and ground cloves. Certain stores carry them loose, but the spices packed in the little commercial cans work just as well.

## Herbs

There's something very mellowing about clipping your own fresh herbs just before adding them to a bread recipe. If you do this, remember to use twice as much as you would if they were dry, and also snip them up well with a scissors for maximum flavor.

## Onions and Garlic

In our recipes we use onions both inside breads and on the crusts.

Everyone loves garlic bread—traditionally garlic mixed with butter and rubbed on bread which is then wrapped in foil and heated before serving. We have included a recipe for it using sweet butter, fresh parsley and oregano. French and Italian breads make the nicest garlic breads. Try it with our Whole Wheat Italian Bread, too.

## Nuts

The main nuts in our recipes are walnuts, pecans, peanuts, and almonds. They can be used whole, chopped, or crushed fine, and add oil, protein, and food value to bread, as well as nutty flavor.

## Fruits

You can use fresh, canned, frozen, or dried fruits, though it's not easy to come by canned or frozen fruits that haven't been artificially colored, flavored, and preserved and so drenched in icky-sweet syrup that you can't tell the pineapples from the kumquats. Canned and frozen fruits must first be drained of liquid.

Raisins, dates, figs, and other dried fruits should first be rolled or dredged in flour before being added to dough to keep them from popping out during kneading. For some soda breads, we'll suggest you soak dried fruits in hot water or milk. In such cases, buttermilk is not necessary to activate the baking soda because the acid from the fruits does the job.

## FATS

There are certain breads, like matzo and some types of French bread, which are made without fats, but in most breads a small amount of fat improves the flavor and makes the dough easier to work with. In yeast breads, fat must be used cautiously, as too much of it can inhibit the growth of yeast and prevent proper fermentation and rising.

Some ingredients like whole milk and finely crushed nuts are rich in fats; so breads using these things may not need much or any extra fat.

A case where fat is essential is in waffles, where butter is lavishly employed to prevent the waffle from sticking to the iron.

### Butter

When our recipes call for butter, we mean sweet butter. Butter comes in many forms: sticks, pounds, sweet, lightly salted, whipped, canned, or churned at home from cream or sour cream. For economy and convenience, we like a good grade of sweet butter packed in $\frac{1}{4}$-pound sticks with a wrapper that gives you tablespoon markings. One stick equals 8 Tbsp or $\frac{1}{2}$

cup. As butter picks up odors easily, wrap it carefully when storing in the refrigerator.

Be sure to reduce the amount of salt in your recipes slightly if you use salted butter rather than sweet.

When you are melting butter, do it slowly, as it can burn easily. If it does, throw it out and start over rather than ruin the flavor of your bread.

## Margarine

For reasons of economy, many people prefer to use margarine in cooking, and you can, if you like, use this substitute wherever you see "butter" in our recipes. Most commercial brands contain excess garbage, however, and we are frankly biased in favor of pure butter.

## Oil

Corn oil is a good choice for corn bread, rye bread, whole wheat bread, and Challah recipes.

Peanut oil burns at a higher temperature than corn oil and is less likely to smoke when used at the recommended temperature for frying doughnuts, and for coating pans and baking sheets.

These two oils, plus butter, did fine for us in all the recipes, but you might like to experiment with some of the other oils— safflower, sunflower seed, sesame seed, walnut, or any other variety of seed or nut oil.

## SUBSTITUTION

Don't be frustrated if you don't have the exact ingredients suggested in a recipe. Substitutions as listed below will work just as well.

1 whole egg = 2 egg yolks

1 cup butter or margarine = $\frac{7}{8}$ cup vegetable oil (1 level cup minus 2 Tbsp)

1 ounce or 1 square unsweetened chocolate = 3 Tbsp cocoa plus 1 Tbsp oil or butter

1 tsp baking powder plus $\frac{1}{2}$ cup sweet whole milk = $\frac{1}{4}$ tsp baking soda plus $\frac{1}{2}$ cup sour milk or buttermilk

1 cup buttermilk or sour milk = 1 cup sweet whole milk plus 1 Tbsp vinegar or lemon juice; or, 1 cup sweet whole milk plus $1\frac{3}{4}$ tsp cream of tartar

1 cup fluid skim milk = 1 cup reconstituted nonfat dry milk

1 cup fluid whole milk = $\frac{1}{2}$ cup evaporated milk plus $\frac{1}{2}$ cup water; or, 1 cup fluid skim milk plus $2\frac{1}{2}$ tsp butter or margarine

*The Tools to Make It With*

Our compiled list of baking tools is fairly extensive and they're not all necessary for a beginner—in fact, you can get by with a large mixing bowl, a wooden spoon, a measuring cup and measuring spoons, a wooden board (the back of a large cheese board sufficed for us first time out) or tabletop, a loaf pan or baking sheet, one oven, and a nail or hand brush—good to use before kneading dough and shaping bread as dough has a tendency to absorb dirt . . . helpful after kneading to remove hardened dough from under nails, off hands, elbows, knees. . . .

However, if you plan to do a lot of bread making, everything on the list comes in handy. Once you have the proper tools, it's difficult to remember how you did without them. (How did we ever get sticky dough off the board without a baker's pastry scraper?)

## EQUIPMENT

Set of Mixing Bowls, plus one Very Large Bowl
Wooden Spoons—don't use the ones you keep for regular use, as those usually taste like onion, garlic, etc.
Standard Measuring Cups including $\frac{1}{4}$ cup, $\frac{1}{3}$ cup, $\frac{1}{2}$ cup, 1 cup, 2 cups, 1 quart. Try to use level measures so you can scrape off excess rather than shake it down
Measuring Spoons—$\frac{1}{4}$ tsp, $\frac{1}{2}$ tsp, 1 tsp, 1 Tbsp
Flour Sifter
Rubber Scraper or Spatula—preferably more than one, if possible
Wire Whisk
Rotary Beater
Electric Blender
Pastry Blender

Baker's Pastry Scraper
Rolling Pins—one long and one short (available in
    various shapes and sizes, 6–18 inches long)
Sharp Knife
Pastry Brush—a fine feather one is best
Bread Board or Table Top—or reverse side of
    Large Carving Board
Spray Bottle or Atomizer
Biscuit Cutters and English Muffin Cutter—to
    make your own, see page 202.
Doughnut Cutter
Cake Tester, Broom Straw, or Wood Toothpick
Large Spoon or Ladle for pancakes and waffles
Saucepans for melting butter, scalding milk,
    heating bagel water or doughnut oil, etc.
Kitchen Timer
Room Thermometer
Oven Thermometer
Deep-frying Thermometer
Tea or Dish Towels
Plastic Wrapping
Baking or Cookie Sheet
Bread Pans—mini: $5\frac{1}{2} \times 3 \times 2$ inches
    small: $8 \times 4 \times 2\frac{1}{4}$ inches
    medium: $8\frac{1}{2} \times 4\frac{1}{2} \times 2\frac{1}{2}$ inches
    large: $9 \times 5 \times 3$ inches
Soufflé Dishes or Pie Plates for round loaves
8-inch Square Pan, plus other square and rect-
    angular pans
Muffin Pan
Popover Pan or Custard Cups for popovers
Cooling Racks
Cast-iron 2-burner Griddle for pancakes, English
    muffins, etc.
Waffle Iron
Nail or Hand Brush

Sturdy metal pans and baking sheets seem to distribute the heat more evenly than glass or coated pans. Glass pans absorb heat very quickly, so your crust may be done to perfection while the inside is still raw. When using them, compensate by setting your oven thermostat 25° lower than the recipe recommends.


## KNOW YOUR OVEN


Naturally, your oven is a very important tool in making bread. It can be a close friend or powerful enemy—turning out creations that do you proud or funny-smelling blackened lumps of charcoal.

Gas heat is more moist than electric because when gas burns the hydrogen in it combines with oxygen in the air and produces water vapor. Your oven, whether gas or electric, will have its own peculiarities. If it is an electric oven you may find it necessary to set your oven 25° lower than the temperatures indicated in our recipes. The first time you try a recipe, watch the bread carefully. If a temperature change is required, note it on the recipe for future use.

Though not always reliable, an inexpensive oven thermometer can be used to test the accuracy of your oven's thermostat. Should the two temperatures greatly disagree have your oven tested and adjusted by a competent professional.

Another way to determine if your oven is hot enough for bread is to sprinkle a tablespoon of flour into a thin, preheated pan and stick it in the oven. If the flour burns or becomes dark brown in a few seconds, the temperature is too high. Turn it down and let the oven cool off before putting in your bread. If the flour doesn't change color at all after a few seconds, the temperature is too low so turn it up. You know the temperature is right when the flour turns slightly brown and looks a little scorched.

The setting of your oven depends on the type of bread to be baked. Dark breads usually require a moderate oven (325°–375°) while light breads need a hotter one (375°–450°). Always place the bread in the upper half or third of a preheated oven (unless instructed differently) so the bottom doesn't brown faster than the rest of the loaf.

A way to simulate a baker's oven is to produce steam. This improves the crust, color, and volume of your bread. Do it by putting a roasting pan on the bottom rack of the oven and partially filling it with boiling water before you put in bread. Or quickly open the oven door during baking and throw a little water onto the floor of the oven—¼ cup or less.

# *Putting It Together*

# TO SIFT OR NOT TO SIFT

The reason you sift flour is to remove lumps and get an accurate measurement. A fairly general rule of thumb for this book is to sift your white flour but use the others unsifted.

Commercial brands of white flour are generally marked presifted but we recommend you resift unbleached white (or all-purpose white) anyway before measuring it into your bowl, as directed in most of the recipes. In a few instances, we don't recommend sifting this flour and say so in the ingredient list with the recipe.

If the recipe directs you to sift whole wheat, rye, oat, or soy flours, before using the flour throw back in any of the bran or grains you sifted out.

When using several flours mix them together thoroughly before combining them with liquid ingredients.


## MIXING, BEATING, KNEADING, CREAMING, BLENDING, FOLDING IN, CUTTING IN, RUBBING IN, AND WHIPPING

These are the techniques used for combining ingredients.

*Mixing*—Combining with a stirring motion at moderate speed.

*Beating*—Combining dry and liquid ingredients in a bowl by vigorously mixing them into a batter with a wooden spoon, wire whisk, or rotary or electric beater. As more and more dry ingredients are added to the batter and it is more and more difficult to beat, it becomes a dough which requires

*Kneading*—Should be done with clean hands, lightly oiled and floured to prevent sticking. The dough is turned out of the bowl onto a lightly floured board and worked by pushing it with the heels of the hands, repeatedly turning and folding it over, until it is smooth and elastic.

*Creaming*—Combining ingredients of different textures, like butter with sugar, with the back of a large spoon, electric beater (slow speed), or fork. It requires a much gentler sort of mixing technique than beating.

*Blending*—Combining ingredients of the same texture with a gentler touch than beating but not as gentle as creaming.

*Folding in*—Combining a lighter mixture, such as beaten egg whites, with a heavier one like waffle or pancake batter. Place the lighter mixture on top of the heavier one and cut down through the middle of both with a spatula. Then draw the spatula toward you, turning the mixture over and turning the bowl, as you do so. Continue till blended.

*Cutting in, Rubbing in*—Usually describes combining firm butter or margarine with flour. To distribute it evenly, chop or rub the butter or margarine into flour with a knife, fork, fingertips, or pastry blender.

*Whipping*—Rapidly beating egg whites, cream, etc., to introduce air and thus lightness.


## RISING


As part of the rising process, you punch the dough down or "cut it back" and then let it rise again. This releases yeast gases and redistributes yeast cells, allowing the dough to continue fermenting. The more risings you allow, the finer and evener your bread's texture will be.

As most of our breads are relatively coarse in texture, two risings—one in the bowl, the next in the loaf pan or on the baking sheet—seem good enough for achieving lightness. If you feel that your bread hasn't come out as light as you'd like, the next time you make it, let it rise twice in the bowl and then again in the pan or on the sheet.

The rising conditions recommended for most breads are a temperature of 70°–80° and a place that is free from drafts and fairly free from traffic. You don't want everybody and the dog knocking against it. Out in the sun on a warm, calm day is fine. But on cold days, place your covered bowl in the unheated oven with a pan of warm water under it or set the covered bowl in a second bowl filled with warm water. Diana's method is to set the covered bowl in a corner on a wooden surface (which insulates it) or on a towel. The only way to be certain of rising temperature is to place a movable room thermometer next to the bread.

Times given for rising in recipes are approximate. Rising for one reason or another may be much quicker or slower. The recipe will indicate whether the bread should "double in bulk" or "triple in bulk." It isn't easy to judge this precisely, but if you've left it longer than you meant to and you find the rising has gotten really out of hand since you last checked it, punch or stir it down and let it rise again to the proper size. Over-risen bread may have an uneven texture, or fall during baking. Bread that is left to rise for several days (we experimented) is likely to develop a hard crust and an off-taste, and is fit for nothing but throwing away.

A technique that slows up the rising process but is convenient and creates a very light, even-textured bread is to do one of your risings overnight in the refrigerator.

To refrigerate a first rising—after kneading the dough, round it up into a ball, place it in a greased bowl, cover it with plastic or a damp towel to lessen drying out, and put it in the refrigerator. Next morning, remove the dough and let it warm to room temperature (15 minutes to 1 hour depending on size of dough, how cold the refrigerator is, etc.), and proceed with the second rising, shaping and baking.

To refrigerate a second rising or after the loaves have been formed, place the loaves on baking sheet, in bread pans, etc., cover carefully with plastic or towels, and refrigerate. The next morning, remove the sheet or pans, let dough warm to room temperature, and proceed with glazing (if desired) and baking.

# TO MAKE A TENT-LIKE COVER
## FOR RISING BREAD

When a loaf of bread is shaped and set to rise before baking it is usually desirable to cover the loaf, to keep it from drying out and to protect it from dust, insects, little people, dogs, etc.

If the dough is sticky, you may want to avoid having the covering material touch the loaf.

To make a tent-like cover, put the bread on a baking sheet (in pans or free standing, as required by your recipe), and at each of the four corners of the baking sheet place a tall water glass.

Then take a large towel or a large sheet of plastic, drape the cover over the glasses, and tuck the edges of the covering material under the edges of the baking sheet. The water glasses act as your tent poles and hold up the cover so it does not touch the bread.

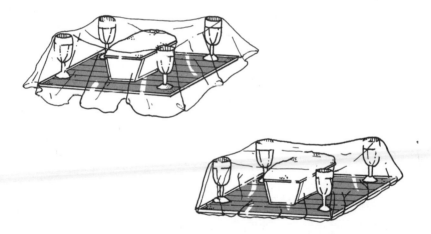

Plastic (the kind that dry cleaners use to cover clean clothes) is particularly convenient to use. You can see through it to tell whether or not the bread has risen as much as the recipe requires without disturbing the cover.

# RESTING

In a number of recipes, we suggest you let the dough rest at various points. This time allows the flour to absorb the liquid and the yeast to become active, which makes the dough more cohesive for kneading, less sticky and more elastic. This period can be from 5 to 20 minutes.

# SHAPING

Just the way breads don't all have to taste the same, they don't have to look the same either. There are traditional shapes for certain breads, but once you get into experimenting with various ones you can make any bread in the form that pleases or amuses you most.

The first three shapings illustrated and described are the ones we use most frequently in our recipes.

### Jelly Roll Shape

Shape the dough into a long rectangle, as wide as the length of the pan. If you are using a baking sheet, make the loaves

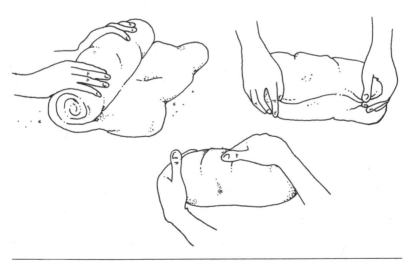

the measurement you wish or as instructed in the recipe. Starting from the shorter side (the pan length) of the rectangle, roll the dough up evenly, pinching seams on the bottom and sides, and tapering into an attractively shaped loaf. Put in prepared bread pan or on baking sheet seam side down. This makes a nice uniformly shaped loaf which can be used for stiff doughs such as those for Italian bread, French bread, pumpernickel, rye, etc.

Well-rounded Oblong Shape

Flatten loaf-size portion of dough into a flat oblong sheet approximately 3 times the width of the pan and as long. Fold the longest end $\frac{1}{3}$ over the center of the dough and press with

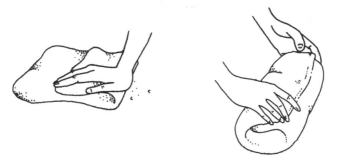

the heel of the hand to seal. Fold the other end over the first seam (like folding a letter) and press down to seal overlap and end seams. Put in pan with the seam side down and press down so that the dough touches the sides. The center of this loaf will be a little higher than ends. This shaping is best for pan loaves such as Joan's Improved Herb Bread, the Cornell Bread, etc.

Round Loaves

After the dough has been sufficiently kneaded, gather it into one or two balls. Turn the dough smooth side up and roll it back and forth between the palms of your hands, tucking a bit of dough under the ball as you rotate it. Tuck and rotate about half a dozen times, turn the dough over, and pinch bottom seams together. Place ball on prepared baking sheet, in pie plate or soufflé dish. This shaping is particularly good for stiff doughs such as pumpernickel, rye, etc.

Round Ring Loaves

Divide your dough in half for 2 loaves and shape each half into a long rope about 20 inches long. Form the rope into a ring, pinching ends together to seal. Round out the middle hole and carefully place it on prepared baking sheet. Let rise. Just before baking, glaze and cut diagonal slashes 1/4 inch deep and about 1 inch apart around rings. This is especially nice for French, Italian, or Cinnamon Spiral dough.

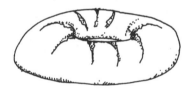

Braiding

Here are two slightly different methods. Choose the one you like better.

*Method 1.* After dividing the dough in half for 2 loaves, and each half into 6 parts, roll each part into a rope about 14 inches long, with the center thicker than the ends. (It usually happens that some are larger than others.) Place 3 of the larger ropes on a lightly greased baking sheet which has been dusted with cornmeal. Hold the ropes at one end and loosely braid them together; fasten them at both ends, pinching them together and tucking ends under. Now braid the 3 smaller ropes together. Place this braid on top of the first. Make sure the ends of the top braid overlap the ends of the bottom braid and pinch them securely together. Repeat this procedure for the other half of your original dough and then follow whatever instructions remain in your recipe.

*Method 2.* After dividing the dough and forming 6 ropes (as in Method 1) lay the 3 larger ropes on a prepared baking sheet. Cross these ropes in the center, braid to each end and pinch ends together. Braid the remaining 3 smaller ropes and place them on the first braid. Overlap them slightly and pinch together. Repeat procedure for the other half of your original dough, following remaining instructions in recipe.

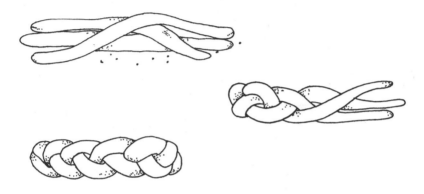

Challah, Boat Style

Divide dough into 2 pieces—one being twice the size of the other. Shape the larger one into an elongated boat shape with tapered ends. Divide the smaller piece into 3 equal portions. Shape these into ropes and braid them as long as the base. Brush the center of the boat with water and place braid on top. After rising, brush entire loaf with cold water before putting into oven. Bake challah with a pan of boiling water on bottom rack of oven. This shaping is good with any challah or fairly stiff dough.

Checkerboard Loaf

Take two different kinds of dough and make 2 strands of each. Lay one kind beside the other; then lay the remaining 2 strands on top of the first 2 in checkerboard fashion. Twist. Put in loaf pan with ends flat against ends of pan (rather than tucking them under). Try this style with braided loaves and Fragrant Light and Dark Bread.

Pull-apart Loaf

Divide dough into small roll-size pieces. Shape into balls. Roll in melted butter and press tightly together in loaf pan. (Alternating between dark and light dough makes an interesting loaf.) If your pan is small, make a single row. If large, a double row. Let rise and bake. This is good with any dough, best with dough containing a lot of wheat flour. When dough has risen, each section will be about the thickness of a good-size slice.

Bubble Loaf

Form the dough into a large ball and then divide into small balls, about 1 inch in diameter. Stack these double in a prepared

bread pan. Cover this with a towel or plastic (if it is left to rise overnight) until the dough almost reaches the top of the pan. Bake according to directions. Any of our yeast-rising recipes can be formed into a bubble loaf. Since the balls of dough aren't oiled or buttered separately before putting them in the pan, they will merge and not pull apart as easily as a pull-apart loaf.

## GLAZING

Glazing is a very simple technique and can give your bread a soft, hard, or very hard crust; or a yellow-brown, red-brown, light, shiny, or dark finish. For dark ryes, we prefer a very dark shiny appearance and hard crust. Corn ryes are nice glazed yellow or golden brown. For white or light breads, we like red-brown in color, with a soft crust. You can try whatever appeals to you. Glazes can also be chosen for your convenience. For example, an egg yolk glaze put on *before* baking is just as good as a cornstarch glaze which has to be cooked and applied when baking is nearly finished.

A good tool to have for glazing is a feather brush or atomizer.

Butter Glaze

Makes a *tender, soft* crust. After baking, brush the bread with melted butter or margarine and cover with a cloth until cool.

---

√

## Water Glaze, Wine Glaze, Whole Egg Glaze

Make *hard* crusts, each of which creates its own characteristic color. Before baking, glaze with water, salt water (1 tsp salt to 1 cup water), white wine (an elegant touch), or 1 whole egg beaten with 1 Tbsp water. A good time to sprinkle on seeds.

## Egg White Glaze

Makes *light, shiny* crusts. An egg white glaze is good for Italian or French bread and rolls. Beat 1 egg white with 1 or 2 Tbsp water or white wine. Brush it over loaf before baking. Good time for seeds or coarse salt.

## Egg Yolk Glaze

Makes *highly glazed brown* crusts. An egg yolk glaze is good for ryes, white breads and challahs. Beat 1 egg yolk with 1 or 2 Tbsp cold water. Brush it over loaf before baking or once before rising and once again before baking. Sprinkle with seeds or diced onion.

## Coffee Glaze

Makes *dark-colored* crusts. This glaze is very good for dark ryes and produces a very dark finish. Mix 1 tsp instant coffee with 2 Tbsp water. Brush on loaf before baking.

## Cornstarch Glaze

Makes *very hard* crusts. This is a very good all-around glaze which we use on many breads. In a saucepan, cook 1 tsp cornstarch with ½ cup water, stirring constantly until thick. About 10 minutes before end of baking time take the loaf out of the oven and brush on the mixture. Return it to the oven 10 minutes more for the crust to harden.

Crackle Glaze

Makes a *shiny, hard* crust with blotches, spots, streaks of different colors. About 10 minutes before your loaf goes into the oven, soak ½ tsp yeast and 1 tsp sugar in 2 Tbsp warm water. When it bubbles, stir in 2 Tbsp arrowroot or cornstarch and 1 tsp oil. Let it stand until just before loaf goes in oven. Then stir down the bubbles and brush the glaze on. As it bakes, the crust will crackle and form a mottled design.

# Hints That Help

## WEATHER, TIME, AND SPACE

Everybody talks about the weather but nobody does anything about it. No longer true. While such conditions used to be of great concern to bread makers—rainy and humid weather tended to foul things up—unless you are living without electricity these things don't matter much. If the room you are working in is hot or steamy or drafty, if you are becoming irritable, uncomfortable, and the dough is sticking to your sweaty hands, take it all into another room or let part of the rising process take place in the refrigerator. Or better yet, take it over to your friend's air-conditioned kitchen.

In her New York apartment's $7 \times 9$-foot kitchen, Diana worked her bread on the kitchen counter. If it became too stuffy or warm there, she moved into the dining room and worked on the dining-room table. Joan's kitchen, around $12 \times 15$ feet, left quite a lot of flailing room.

*Once you select a recipe, read it all the way through.* That way you'll have a good idea of ingredients, methods of mixing and shaping, and time allotment. You don't want to be involved with a bread that needs your attention in 40 minutes when you're going to cook dinner in 30 minutes.

## STORING FLOUR

If you plan to bake a lot, keep your flour in a place near your preparation and baking area. A simple, open bookshelf arrangement in the kitchen works well, where flours can be stored in 1-, 2-, and 3-pound coffee cans (which now generally come with good, tight plastic tops), painted on the outside *only*, with lead-free paint, and labeled in large, clear letters.

If you're storing flour and other ingredients at a cooler temperature (like in the refrigerator or cellar), they must be warmed to room temperature before using, as cold ingredients drastically slow down rising (whole wheat and rye breads take enough time under room-temperature circumstances, so they need all the help they can get).

## FAUNA IN YOUR FLOUR

Sooner or later you are likely to encounter the flour weevil, a small, dark-colored oblong insect about pinhead size. Do not panic! Weevils are harmless, do not carry disease, and usually arrive in your kitchen clinging to the outside of flour bags, where they have been lapping up spilled flour.

To prevent weevils and their kin from permanent residency, store each new flour purchase in a tightly sealed plastic bag or container which has been carefully washed before using. And keep your storage area clean and free of spills.

Sometimes you find a grub or two. These are small, white, and wormlike. If you find just a couple in your flour, simply remove them from the premises. If you find many, remove your flour from the premises as well. The best way to avoid grubs is to buy flour from places which do a high volume of business and consequently carry relatively fresh flour, or from stores which date their flour.

## STORING FRESH BREAD

Wrap or store your bread as soon as it's cooled.

It seems homemade bread keeps so well, you only have to put it in a clean, well-aired bread box, a tin, or a plastic bag for proper storing. Because bread dries out more quickly when refrigerated, don't do so unless your kitchen is extremely warm (in which case mold may form).

Freezing extra loaves is a good idea when you want to have a lot of homemade bread without baking every day. To store your bread in the freezer, either slice it or keep it whole and wrap it in plastic bags or freezer wrap.

# REFRESHING BREAD

Defrost frozen breads in wrapper or plastic bag so they won't dry out and then place in a 400° oven for about 10 minutes. Or, wrap the frozen bread in aluminum foil. Open one end to allow moisture to escape and the crust to harden and bake at 400° for 20 minutes.

Refresh yeast breads, particularly rye, pumpernickel, and Black Bread (either homemade or store-bought) by spraying them with a little water, then placing in a hot oven (around 400°) for 20 minutes. Cool and serve. Spray French and Italian breads with a little water, wrap in aluminum foil (keep one end open for steam to escape), bake in a 400° oven until soft (15–20 minutes), and serve hot.

Muffins, rolls, and buttery bread should not be covered but heated quickly in a hot oven.

# ADDED INFINITUMS

## Sticky Fingers and How Not to Have Them

You'll find dough sticks to your fingers on days when your hands are very dry and have been in a lot of water. Cut this down by pouring some oil on your hands and rubbing it in. Wipe off any excess oil with a paper towel. Before plunging your hands into the dough, stick them into flour.

Rubbing oil into your board will help keep the dough from sticking to it.

## Reserve Some Flour

When mixing your dry ingredients together, reserve about ½–1 cup flour from the total amount in the recipe, using it on the board and for kneading. Add still more if dough remains sticky after the reserve has been kneaded in. It is near impossible to give an exact amount of flour in a recipe, as flours vary according to grade, absorbability, and kneading technique used.

## Half Fill Bread Pans

Fill your bread pans just half full to allow the bread room to expand without billowing over the sides, down the pan, and onto the racks and the oven bottom, making baking a big cleanup hassle. If your bread is ready for the oven and the pan is more than half full, put the dough into a larger pan or two smaller ones. The extra effort will be worthwhile later on.

## One More Note to the Novice

There's nothing more encouraging than baking a near-perfect bread first time out. The first yeast bread recipe in this book is a good one to start you off—Joan's Improved Herb Bread. It's simple to get together and delicious to eat. When you knead it, watch it rise, fit it into the loaf pans, smell it baking, then slice it, butter it, and pass it around still warm from the oven —you'll know the power of making your own bread!

# Yeast Breads

# YEAST BREAD SCENARIO

Read through recipe and assemble all ingredients and equipment required. Sift flour if necessary.

1. Using 1-cup measure or small container, sprinkle required amount of yeast into ¼ or ½ cup water, body temperature. Stir and set aside.

2. In large or medium-size bowl combine all flours. Remove and reserve ½–1 cup for kneading in as directed. Add other dry ingredients such as salt, sugar, wheat germ, brewer's yeast. Add fruits, nuts, seeds; mix to dredge with flour so they won't stick together or pop out when kneading dough.

3. In third container mix remainder of liquid ingredients such as melted butter, oil, melted chocolate, molasses, honey, slightly beaten egg(s), scalded milk cooled to body temperature, additional water, etc.

4. Combine liquid ingredients with yeast mixture in large bowl. Add combined dry ingredients (or as directed in recipe). Beat with wooden spoon until dough starts to come away from sides of bowl. Add more flour and knead in bowl, until dough begins to form a ball. Turn out on lightly floured board and let dough rest while you wash, dry, and grease or oil bowl (ready

for Step 6). A longer rest period may be suggested in recipe. Purpose of rest period is to let flour absorb as much moisture as possible. Dough will be less sticky and will have started to rise a tiny bit.

5. Oil and flour your hands and knead dough by folding

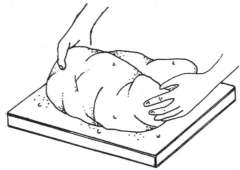

toward you, then pushing it down and away from you with heels of your hands. If you move your body forward and back,

the rocking movement will be soothing and more comfortable than just working with your arms. Give dough a quarter turn and repeat procedure, adding more flour as necessary, until dough is smooth, elastic, and doesn't stick to board. The purpose of kneading is to make sure dough is well mixed, of even texture, smooth, and to develop its elasticity. If dough continues to stick, scrape it up with baker's pastry scraper, rub a little oil into board, flour lightly, and try again.

6. When kneaded dough is smooth and elastic, round it up into ball, pinching out air bubbles and creases, and place in

greased bowl. Roll dough around in bowl until well greased. Cover with towel and let rise in warm place (70°–80°) free from drafts for about 1 hour or until double in bulk. (You can use a movable room thermometer to check temperature.)

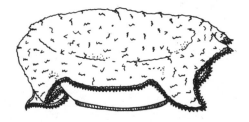

7. The dough has risen enough when two fingers poked into dough leave indentations that do not spring back.

8. Punch dough down by pushing fist into dough as far as it will go about 10 times. Dough will not go down to its original size before rising. Re-form into ball, cover, and let rise second time; or turn out onto lightly floured board to shape loaves. Using sharp knife, divide dough in half (or as directed in recipe).

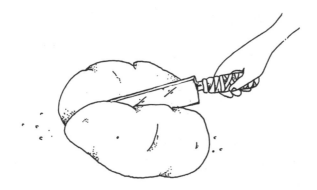

9. Use jelly roll shape to make loaf for bread pan. Roll each half of dough into rectangle with rolling pin, making short side of rectangle same dimension as desired length of loaf. Starting from short side, roll dough up evenly, pinching seams on bottom and sides, and tapering to form attractively shaped loaf. Repeat with other half of dough. (To make long loaf, such as French bread, roll dough from long side of rectangle.) Lightly grease bread pans or baking sheet and sprinkle with cornmeal

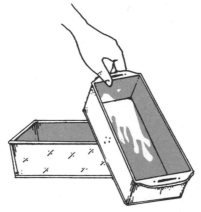

or seeds, tilting to spread evenly. Put loaves, seam side down, in bread pans or on baking sheet, cover, and let rise in warm place (70°–80°) free from drafts until double in bulk. Rising may take from 30 minutes to several hours. (See page 49.)

10. Glaze and slash loaves, or not, as directed in recipe.

---

11. Preheat oven.

12. Put risen loaves in oven and bake 1 hour, or as directed, until done. (Cover loaves that are browning too fast with brown paper or aluminum foil.) Test by thumping bread with knuckle. Loaves are done if they sound hollow.

13. Remove loaves from pans immediately—don't they look good! Try to cool on rack for a little while before eating.

*In our recipes, a large loaf pan is 9 × 5 × 3 inches, a medium loaf pan is 8½ × 4½ × 2½ inches, a small loaf pan is 8 × 4 × 2¼ inches, and a mini pan is 5½ × 3 × 2 inches.*

# Whole Wheat Breads

# JOAN'S IMPROVED HERB BREAD

*Makes 2 large loaves.* Bread is deliciously flavored with cloves and dill.

*Note*: For the beginner, we are giving this opening recipe with every step fully described.

| | |
|---:|:---|
| 2 | cups scalded milk, cooled to body temperature |
| 2 | Tbsp oil |
| 3 | Tbsp honey |
| 1 | tsp dried sage or 2 tsp chopped fresh sage |
| ½ | tsp dried marjoram or 1 tsp chopped fresh marjoram |
| 1 | Tbsp dried dill weed or 2 Tbsp chopped fresh dill |
| ½ | tsp ground cloves |
| 1 | Tbsp salt |
| 2 | Tbsp melted butter |
| 1 | Tbsp or pkg dry yeast |
| ¼ | cup water, body temperature |
| 2 | cups sifted unbleached white flour or white flour with wheat germ |
| ¼ | cup soy flour |
| 2½–3½ | cups whole wheat flour |
| ½ | cup yellow or black raisins |
| | Cornmeal |
| | *Glaze*: 1 Tbsp melted butter |

In large bowl combine 2 cups scalded milk which has been cooled to body temperature, 2 Tbsp oil, 3 Tbsp honey, all herbs and spices, 1 Tbsp salt, and 2 Tbsp melted butter.

In separate small bowl or cup sprinkle 1 Tbsp or pkg dry yeast over ¼ cup water, body temperature; stir and set aside.

In third bowl combine and mix well 2 cups white flour, ¼ cup soy flour, 2½ cups whole wheat flour and ½ cup raisins. (The additional cup whole wheat flour—and you may need even more—will be used on bread board or tabletop when you knead dough to proper consistency).

Add yeast-water mixture to milk-spice mixture. Add combined flour and raisins to liquid mixture, a little at a time. Stir and beat until dough starts to leave sides of bowl. Turn onto lightly floured board. Cover with bowl and let rest 10 minutes.

Knead by folding dough toward you, then punching down and away from you with heels of hands. Give dough a quarter turn and repeat procedure. Continue kneading in this fashion for about 10 minutes, or until dough is smooth and elastic, adding more whole wheat flour as necessary. Form smooth ball, pinching out air bubbles and creases, and place in lightly greased bowl, turning dough to grease entire surface. Cover with towel and let rise in warm place (70°–80°) free from drafts for about 1 hour, or until double in bulk. (When two fingers poked into dough leave indentations that do not spring back, rising is sufficient.)

Punch dough down with fist several times, pressing gas out. Turn dough out onto lightly floured board and divide in half.

Flatten each half of dough into rectangle as long as pan and about 3 times as wide. Starting at short side, roll each rectangle jelly roll fashion and pinch seams on bottom and ends to seal.

Lightly grease 2 large bread pans and sprinkle with cornmeal. Place loaves in pans and brush tops with 1 Tbsp melted butter.

Cover pans and let rise in warm place (70°–80°) free from drafts until double in bulk, or until sides of dough reach tops of pans (about 1 hour). Bake in preheated 400° oven for about 50 minutes to 1 hour. Bread should sound hollow when rapped with knuckle. Remove from pans immediately and cool on wire racks.

# CORNELL WHOLE WHEAT BREAD

*Makes 2 medium loaves.* Besides being delicious to eat (it tastes something like Whole Wheat Batter Bread but is finer-textured and less likely to fall), this recipe offers balanced, satisfying nutrition. It was adapted from one developed at Cornell University.

|        |                              |
|--------|------------------------------|
| 2      | Tbsp or pkgs dry yeast       |
| 2      | cups water, body temperature |
| ¼      | cup molasses                 |
| ¼      | cup light brown sugar        |
| 4–4½   | cups whole wheat flour       |
| 1      | egg, slightly beaten         |
| ½      | cup soy flour                |
| ¾      | cup nonfat dry milk          |
| ¼      | cup wheat germ               |
| ¼      | cup brewer's yeast           |
| 2      | tsp salt                     |
|        | Cornmeal                     |
|        | *Glaze*: 1 Tbsp melted butter (optional) |

In large bowl stir 2 Tbsp or pkgs dry yeast into 2 cups water, body temperature. Mix in ¼ cup molasses and ¼ cup light brown sugar with lumps broken up. Set aside.

Measure out 3 cups whole wheat flour; add to yeast mixture along with 1 egg, slightly beaten, and beat 3 minutes with electric beater or 100 strokes by hand.

In separate container mix together 1 cup whole wheat flour (reserving ½ cup to be worked in later), ½ cup soy flour, ¾ cup nonfat dry milk, ¼ cup wheat germ, ¼ cup brewer's yeast, and 2 tsp salt. Pour into yeast mixture and stir vigorously with wooden spoon until dough begins to leave sides of bowl, adding more whole wheat flour if necessary.

Turn out onto kneading surface and knead about 10 minutes,

adding additional whole wheat flour to gain moderately stiff dough.

Wash, dry, and grease bowl. Round up dough into ball and put in bowl, rolling dough around in bowl until well greased. Cover with towel and let rise in warm place (70°–80°) free from drafts, until doubled in bulk (1 hour or more).

Punch dough down, and if you have time, round up dough and let rise second time, covered, in warm place. If you are in a hurry, skip this second rising, but it improves texture of bread.

After second rising, punch dough down again and turn out onto board. Cut dough in half with sharp knife and shape each half into rectangular loaf. Put loaves in greased medium-size loaf pans which have been sprinkled with cornmeal on bottoms and sides. Cover pans and let loaves rise in warm place (70°–80°) until double in bulk, or about ½ inch from top of pan (45 minutes or longer).

Preheat oven to 350°. Bake 1 hour or until loaves sound hollow when rapped with knuckle. Turn out of bread pans and cool on rack. Brush tops with melted butter for soft crust.

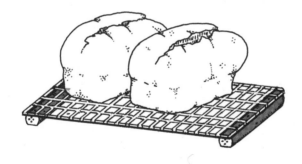

# REFRIGERATOR WHOLE WHEAT BREAD

*Makes 2 medium loaves.* When a progressive three-year-old was offered this bread, he said, "Ah, cake!" and ate two pieces without butter. It's a satisfying daily bread, good with cheese, too.

|     |     |
|----:|-----|
| 6–8 | cups whole wheat flour (about 2 pounds), divided into 2-cup portions |
| 2 | Tbsp or pkgs dry yeast |
| 2 | Tbsp brown sugar or molasses, as you prefer |
| 1 | Tbsp salt |
| ⅔ | cup nonfat dry milk |
| 2½ | cups very warm tap water (120°, or as hot as your hand can comfortably stand) |
| ¼ | cup butter, melted or room temperature |
|   | Cornmeal |
|   | *Glaze:* 1 Tbsp melted butter or corn oil |

An electric mixer or electric hand mixer is convenient to use with this recipe. If you don't have one, or don't like to use the mixer, simply beat well by hand with wooden spoon instead.

In large warm bowl place 2 cups whole wheat flour, 2 Tbsp or pkgs dry yeast, 2 Tbsp brown sugar with lumps broken up, or molasses, 1 Tbsp salt, and ⅔ cup nonfat dry milk. Stir well.

Add 2½ cups very warm water (120° or as hot as your hand can comfortably stand) and ¼ cup soft or melted butter. Mix for 2 minutes with electric mixer at medium speed, scraping sides of bowl from time to time with spatula.

Add 2 more cups of whole wheat flour and mix with electric mixer at high speed for 1 minute more, or until well blended and thick, scraping sides of bowl occasionally.

Stir in 2 cups more whole wheat flour with wooden spoon, and if necessary, additional whole wheat flour until dough leaves sides of bowl.

Turn onto kneading surface and knead in as much additional flour as required to make reasonably stiff dough. Then knead for about 10 minutes, until dough is smooth and very elastic.

Cover with bowl and let rest 20 minutes. Then punch down and cut dough in half with sharp knife. Shape into loaves and place in well-greased medium-size bread pans sprinkled with cornmeal on sides and bottom. Brush tops of loaves with melted butter or corn oil.

Cover pans loosely with plastic and put into refrigerator for 2–24 hours.

When ready to bake, take from refrigerator and let stand uncovered for 10 minutes at room temperature while preheating oven to 400°. Bake 50 minutes to 1 hour, or until loaves sound hollow when rapped with knuckles. Take from pans immediately and cool on wire racks.

## NIEUW AMSTERDAM GRAHAM BREAD

*Makes 2 medium loaves.* This recipe for delicious bread is derived from one given to us by the chief baker of the ship *Nieuw Amsterdam.*

|  |  |
|---|---|
| 2½–3 | cups whole wheat graham flour |
| 2½–3 | cups sifted unbleached white flour |
| 3 | Tbsp or pkgs dry yeast |
| ¾ | cup water, body temperature |
| 3 | Tbsp melted butter or oil |
| 1 | Tbsp malt syrup or dark molasses |
| 1 | cup water, slightly warmer than body temperature |
| 1 | Tbsp salt |
|  | Cornmeal |

Mix together 2½ cups whole wheat graham flour and 2½ cups white flour. Mix together remaining ½ cups as needed. Set aside.

In small container sprinkle 3 Tbsp or pkgs yeast over ¾ cup water, body temperature. Stir and set aside.

Stir 3 Tbsp melted butter or oil and 1 Tbsp malt syrup or molasses into 1 cup water, warmed to slightly more than body temperature. (Use malt syrup if you prefer a slightly bitter, rich flavor to the sweeter molasses flavor.)

In large bowl combine liquid ingredients. Mix 1 Tbsp salt with 1 cup of whole wheat–white flour mixture, and add to liquid ingredients. Beat until smooth. Continue adding flour, beating mixture until dough starts to leave sides of bowl. Turn dough out onto well-floured board, cover, and let rest for 20 minutes.

Knead dough until smooth and elastic, adding more flour until dough is fairly stiff and not too sticky. Shape into ball and place in greased bowl. Roll dough around in bowl until well greased. Cover and let rise in warm place (70°–80°) until double in bulk (about 3 hours).

Punch dough down, turn out onto board, divide in half, and form loaves. Put loaves in greased medium-size bread pans sprinkled with cornmeal and cover with plastic. Let rise second time until double or a little more, about 3 hours. (Try putting in unheated oven with pan of warm water beneath bread pans.)

Bake in preheated 375° oven for about 1 hour or until loaves sound hollow when thumped. Remove from pans and cool on racks.

# MRS. MANN'S BEAUTIFUL LOAF

*Makes 2 medium loaves.* This recipe for whole wheat bread is slightly adapted from one submitted by Mrs. Mary Jane Mann of Victor, New York, "in the interest of good bread making and with the hope that others may benefit."

1¾   cups scalded milk,
          cooled to body temperature
¼   cup butter
¼   cup molasses
1   Tbsp honey
1   egg, slightly beaten (optional)
1   Tbsp or pkg dry yeast
¼   cup water, body temperature
5–5½   cups whole wheat flour
½   cup wheat germ
1   Tbsp salt
    Cornmeal
    *Glaze*: 1 egg white mixed with 2 Tbsp water or
          Cornstarch Glaze (see page 56)

In saucepan scald 1¾ cups milk. Add ¼ cup or ½ stick butter, ¼ cup molasses, and 1 Tbsp honey. Set aside to cool to body temperature. When cooled add 1 slightly beaten egg (optional).

In small container sprinkle 1 Tbsp or pkg dry yeast over ¼ cup water, body temperature. Stir and set aside in warm place until bubbly.

In large bowl combine 4½ cups whole wheat flour, ½ cup wheat germ, and 1 Tbsp salt. Add bubbling yeast mixture and cooled milk mixture. Beat dough with wooden spoon until flour is blended and dough starts to leave sides of bowl. Turn out on lightly floured board. Knead in additional flour as necessary until dough is no longer sticky and is somewhat stiff, about 10 minutes. Let dough rest while you wash, dry, and grease

---

bowl. Round dough up into ball, put it back into greased bowl, turning so that it is well greased, cover, and let rise in a warm place (70°–80°) free from drafts until double in bulk (several hours).

Punch down. Turn out and divide in half. Form into loaves and place on greased baking sheet or in medium-size bread pans sprinkled with cornmeal. Cover and let rise until double in bulk (several hours or overnight, depending on how slow the bread is rising).

Brush with egg white glaze and bake in preheated 350° oven for about 1 hour. Or brush with Cornstarch Glaze during last 10 minutes of baking. Remove from pans and cool on racks.

# White Breads

# BILLOWY WHITE BREAD

*Makes 3 large loaves or 4 medium loaves.* If you are a white-bread buff this is a good bread for everyday with plenty of food value and lots of protein.

½ cup water, body temperature
1 Tbsp or pkg dry yeast
⅔ cup nonfat dry milk plus 1¾ cup boiling
    water (or substitute 2 cups scalded skim or
    scalded whole milk cooled to body temperature)
½ cup melted butter
½ cup light brown sugar
1 Tbsp salt
¼ cup soy flour
7 cups sifted unbleached white flour
¼ cup wheat germ
3 eggs, slightly beaten (reserve 2 Tbsp for glazing)
    *Glaze*: 2 Tbsp egg mixed with 2 Tbsp milk

In cup or small mixing bowl combine ½ cup water, body temperature, and 1 Tbsp or pkg dry yeast. Stir and set aside.

In large mixing bowl put ⅔ cup nonfat dry milk and pour over it 1¾ cups boiling water. (Or substitute 2 cups scalded skim or scalded whole milk.) Add ½ cup melted butter, ½ cup light brown sugar, and 1 Tbsp salt. Stir to dissolve and set aside to cool to body temperature.

Sift into medium-size mixing bowl ¼ cup soy flour and 7 cups white flour. Add ¼ cup wheat germ and mix thoroughly.

Beat 3 eggs in separate bowl; set aside 2 Tbsp of beaten egg for glaze. When milk mixture in large mixing bowl has cooled to body temperature, add eggs and yeast mixture, stirring thoroughly.

Add mixed flours all at once to liquid mixture and stir with wooden spoon until slightly sticky ball of dough is formed.

Turn out onto well-floured bread board and knead 2 or 3

times. Let dough rest while you wash, dry and grease mixing bowl. Then knead dough for 5–6 minutes or until smooth. To make this moist bread, final dough should be slightly sticky so avoid working in too much flour.

Form dough into smooth ball and place in bowl greased with butter, turning dough so that it is well greased. Cover bowl with cloth and let rise in warm place (70°–80°) free from drafts until double in bulk, about 1 hour.

Punch dough down in bowl; re-form into ball, cover, and let rise second time.

Punch dough down again in bowl and turn out onto board. Divide dough into 3 or 4 pieces, depending on whether you are using 3 large or 4 medium-size bread pans. Shape loaves and place into lightly greased bread pans.

Cover and let rise third time until dough doubles in bulk or reaches to within 1 inch of top of bread pans. Mix reserved 2 Tbsp egg with 2 Tbsp milk to make glaze and gently brush tops of loaves (a feather brush is good for this purpose).

Turn oven on (let fumes escape if using gas) and put in bread at once. Set oven at 400° and time for 15 minutes; then lower heat to 375° and continue baking for 25 minutes more or until dark brown and bread sounds hollow when rapped with knuckle. Remove to rack and cool.

*Challah* is a traditional Jewish bread, generally baked before sundown on Friday, when the holy day begins. In Orthodox Jewish circles, the lighting of stoves is not permitted on *Shabbat*.

Anyway, it is delicious baked anytime—a chewy white bread rich in eggs and baked to a beautiful golden-brown braid.

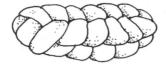

# COOKIE'S REFRIGERATOR CHALLAH

*Makes 2 medium loaves.* Cookie donated this recipe, which comes from a busy rabbi's wife who never has time to complete the whole process in one day. Begin preparation on Wednesday for *Shabbat*.

6–6½ cups sifted unbleached white flour
½ cup soy flour
½ cup light brown sugar
2 tsp salt
2 Tbsp or pkgs dry yeast
2 eggs, slightly beaten
¼ cup oil
2 cups water, body temperature
 Cornmeal
 Poppy seeds
 *Glaze*: 1 egg yolk mixed with 2 Tbsp water

*First day.* In large bowl combine 6 cups white flour, ½ cup soy flour, ½ cup light brown sugar with lumps broken up, 2 tsp salt, and 2 Tbsp or pkgs dry yeast. Mix thoroughly.

Beat 2 eggs slightly, add ¼ cup oil and beat together; add to dry ingredients. Stir with wooden spoon, gradually adding 2 cups water, body temperature. Work dough until it starts to come away from sides of bowl. Turn out onto lightly floured board and knead until smooth, elastic, and glistening, adding more flour as necessary to gain this consistency. Form dough into ball. Wash, dry, and oil bowl. Place dough in bowl, turning so that dough is well oiled. Cover with plastic and refrigerate 24 hours.

*Second day.* Punch dough down, fold in outside crust, reform into ball, cover, and let rise again overnight in refrigerator.

*Next morning.* Turn dough out onto floured bread board

and punch down. Knead 5 minutes. With sharp knife, divide dough in half. Now divide each half into 6 pieces, 3 slightly larger than other 3. Let rest 10 minutes. Roll each piece to make rope about 14 inches long, with center of rope thicker than ends. Select 3 larger ropes and place on lightly oiled baking sheet dusted with cornmeal. Braid loosely; pinch ends together and tuck under (see "Shaping," page 49).

Make another braid of 3 smaller ropes and place second braid on top of large braid. Secure, making sure ends of top braid overlap ends of bottom braid.

Repeat procedure with second half of dough. Brush loaves with beaten egg yolk mixed with 2 Tbsp water and sprinkle with poppy seeds.

Cover loaves with tent-like covering (see page 48) and let rise in warm place (70°–80°) free from drafts until a little more than double in bulk. Bake in preheated 375° oven for 45 minutes to 1 hour, or until golden brown. Tap bottom and top braids; if they sound hollow, loaves are done. Remove to rack and cool.


## JOAN'S CHALLAH

*Makes 1 giant loaf.* This "Holly"—the way they always pronounced it in Joan's family—is a single-braid bread rather than a double.

|       |                                       |
|------:|---------------------------------------|
| 3     | Tbsp or pkgs dry yeast                |
| 2     | cups water, body temperature          |
| 3     | eggs, beaten (reserve 2 Tbsp for glazing) |
| 1/2   | cup light honey                       |
| 1¾    | cups oil                              |
| 4     | tsp salt                              |
| About 7 | cups sifted unbleached white flour  |
| 1     | Tbsp poppy seeds                      |
|       | *Glaze*: 2 Tbsp egg                   |

In very large bowl sprinkle 3 Tbsp or pkgs dry yeast over 2 cups water, body temperature. Stir and set aside.

In separate container beat 3 eggs (set aside 2 Tbsp for glazing) ; beat in ½ cup honey and 1¾ cups oil. Add to yeast mixture in large bowl. Add 4 tsp salt and about 6 cups white flour 1 cup at a time, stirring until dough starts to form ball and leave sides of bowl.

Turn dough onto lightly floured board, knead about 10 minutes or until smooth, adding more flour as needed. Form into ball and place in oiled bowl, turning so that dough is well oiled. Cover and let rise in warm place (70°–80°) free from drafts 1 hour or until double in bulk. Punch down and place on floured board.

With sharp knife, divide dough into 3 equal portions. Roll into snaky strips about 18 inches long. Braid strips together and seal ends. Place on oiled baking sheet. Let rise in warm place (70°–80°) 1 hour, or until double in bulk.

Brush challah with reserved egg. Sprinkle with poppy seeds. Place in preheated 350° oven and bake for 1 hour or until golden brown.

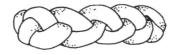

# French, Italian, and American Long Loaf Breads

# WHOLE WHEAT ITALIAN BREAD

*Makes 2 loaves.* This is a fine-textured Italian bread with a really different taste.

<pre>
    1   Tbsp or pkg dry yeast
    2   cups water, body temperature
    1   Tbsp light brown sugar
    1   Tbsp salt
   ¼    cup wheat germ
   ¼    cup soy flour
  2½    cups whole wheat flour
 3–3½   cups sifted unbleached white flour
    1   Tbsp melted butter
        Cornmeal
        Glaze: 1 egg white mixed with 2 Tbsp
           water or white wine
</pre>

In small bowl or cup sprinkle 1 Tbsp or pkg dry yeast over 2 cups water, body temperature. Stir and set aside.

In large bowl mix 1 Tbsp light brown sugar with lumps broken up, 1 Tbsp salt, ¼ cup wheat germ, ¼ cup soy flour, 2½ cups whole wheat flour, and 2½ cups white flour. Add 1 Tbsp melted butter and yeast solution. Beat with wooden spoon until dough is smooth and stiff and begins to leave sides of bowl.

Turn dough out onto lightly floured board or tabletop. Cover with bowl and let rest for about 15 minutes. Knead dough, adding remaining white flour as necessary to gain smooth and elastic consistency, about 15 minutes.

Place dough in lightly greased bowl, turning dough in bowl until well greased. Cover with damp cloth and let rise in warm place (70°–80°) free from drafts until double in bulk, about 1½ hours.

Punch dough down with fist. Turn onto lightly floured bread board or tabletop. Take sharp knife and divide dough in half.

Flatten each half into rectangle 8 × 16 inches. Beginning at wider end, roll dough into 16-inch loaf, tapering ends. Seal edges and ends by pinching together and smoothing. Roll back and forth, firming, tapering, and lengthening loaves as necessary.

Place prepared loaves, seam side down, on lightly greased baking sheet sprinkled with cornmeal. Brush loaves with egg white slightly beaten with 2 Tbsp water or white wine.

Cover loaves with tent-like covering (see page 48) and let rise in warm place (70°–80°) free from drafts until double in bulk, about 1½ hours.

Preheat oven to 350°. Place pan of boiling water in lower half of oven. With sharp knife gently slash tops of loaves from end to end, ½ inch deep. Place loaves in upper half or middle of oven. Bake 20 minutes and quickly brush loaves again with egg white mixture; continue baking for total time of 50 minutes to 1 hour, or until loaves sound hollow when thumped with knuckle. Cool on wire rack.


## ✓ ALICE'S GARLIC BREAD

Excellent with lunch or dinner.

        1    loaf Italian bread
        ¼    pound whipped butter, softened
        ½    cup minced parsley
        2    medium garlic cloves put through garlic press
             Pinch of oregano

Cut bread in crosswise slices almost all the way through. With fork, stir together ¼ pound whipped butter, ½ cup minced parsley, 2 pressed garlic cloves and pinch of oregano. Spread mixture on each side of bread slices. Wrap loaf in foil and place in preheated 350° oven for 20 minutes. Serve hot.

# ✓ IMPROVED FRENCH BREAD

*Makes 3 loaves.* This recipe involves 3 risings for best results. We believe it tastes better and is more nutritious than any commercial French bread you'll find in *any* country!

|  |  |
|---|---|
| 1 | Tbsp or pkg dry yeast |
| 1⅓ | cups water, body temperature |
| 3–3¾ | cups sifted unbleached white flour |
| ¼ | cup soy flour |
| 2 | Tbsp wheat germ |
| 1 | Tbsp melted butter |
| 1½ | Tbsp light brown sugar |
| 1 | Tbsp salt |
|  | Cornmeal |
|  | *Glaze:* 1 tsp salt dissolved in 1 cup cold water |

Sprinkle 1 Tbsp or pkg dry yeast into ⅓ cup water, body temperature. Stir and set aside.

Into large mixing bowl put 3 cups white flour, ¼ cup soy flour, and 2 Tbsp wheat germ; stir together.

In another bowl, mix 1 cup water, body temperature, 1 Tbsp melted butter, 1½ Tbsp light brown sugar, and 1 Tbsp salt. Add yeast mixture and stir.

Combine liquid and dry mixtures and stir with wooden spoon until well blended. Add additional white flour until moist, slightly sticky dough ball is formed, then turn out onto lightly floured board. Let dough rest while you wash, dry, and grease mixing bowl.

Knead dough about 10 minutes, until smooth and elastic. It will still be slightly sticky and moist. Form dough into smooth ball and place in greased bowl, turning over 2 or 3 times to grease all sides. Cover with damp cloth and put in warm place free from drafts with temperature below 80°. For this bread to have its best taste and texture, rising should not happen too fast; 70°–75° is preferable. Let rise until double or triple in bulk—about 1 hour or more.

---

Punch down dough, form into ball again, and let rise second time, covered, until double or triple in bulk.

Turn dough onto lightly floured board and punch down. Knead a few times; dough will be moist, elastic, and pleasant to touch.

Grease large baking sheet and sprinkle with cornmeal.

Divide dough into thirds by cutting with sharp knife. Roll out one third of dough with rolling pin into thin rectangle about $8 \times 16$ inches. Starting on long side of rectangle, roll up, jelly roll fashion, to make thin, 16-inch-long loaf. Seal edges and ends by pinching together firmly. Loaf will be very thin. Place on baking sheet, seam side down, and cover with damp cloth. Form second and third loaves in same manner and place on baking sheet, leaving 3 inches between loaves.

With very sharp knife make 3 diagonal slashes, $\frac{1}{4}$ inch deep, on top of each loaf, or one slash from end to end.

Cover loaves again with damp cloth, making tent-like covering (see page 48), and let rise until double in bulk, about 30 minutes. Again, be sure temperature is in 70°–75° range.

Preheat oven to 400° and place pan of steaming hot water on bottom rack of oven.

Spray or gently brush risen loaves with cold salt water (1 tsp salt to 1 cup water), but use mixture sparingly. Put loaves in preheated 400° oven. After 15 minutes, *very* gently spray or brush loaves again with cold salt water; repeat 15 minutes later.

Bake until golden, and until loaves sound hollow when rapped with knuckle. Total baking time will be 45 minutes to 1 hour. Remove from oven and cool on wire rack.

---

*Yeast Breads*

# ✓ SOURDOUGH STARTER

| 1 | Tbsp or pkg dry yeast |
|---|---|
| 2¼ | cups water, body temperature |
| 2 | tsp sugar (white or brown) |
| 2¼ | cups unsifted unbleached white flour |

In a large glass bowl or plastic container, with wooden spoon, stir 1 Tbsp or pkg dry yeast into ½ cup water, body temperature. Add 2 tsp sugar. Beat in 2 cups white flour and 1½ cups water, body temperature.

Cover with damp cloth and allow mixture to ferment 5 days in warm place (70°–80°), stirring mixture down each day with wooden spoon and moistening cloth from time to time. On fifth day add ¼ cup flour and ¼ cup water, body temperature, to starter and beat vigorously. Cover and allow to continue fermentation until next day.

On sixth day starter is ready to use, or it may be stored in refrigerator, preferably in glass container with tight-fitting top. Starter should be shaken or stirred daily.

When you use starter, always replace the removed amount with equal amounts of flour and water, body temperature. This is known as feeding. Like, if you're removing 1 cup starter, replace it with 1 cup flour and 1 cup water, body temperature.

If you do not use starter regularly, it should be fed about once a week. Either add 1 tsp sugar and stir well, or remove some of starter and feed it with equal amounts of flour and water.

# SOURDOUGH FRENCH BREAD

*Makes 3 loaves.* This recipe involves 3 risings, to make really delicious, chewy French bread.

|      |                                       |
|------|---------------------------------------|
| 1    | cup sourdough starter                 |
| 1    | Tbsp white vinegar                    |
| 1    | tsp salt                              |
| 3½–4 | cups sifted unbleached white flour    |
| ¾    | cup water, body temperature           |
|      | Cornmeal                              |
|      | *Glaze:* 1 egg white mixed with 1 Tbsp water or white wine |

Combine and mix 1 cup sourdough starter, 1 Tbsp white vinegar, 1 tsp salt and 3 cups white flour. Add ¾ cup water, body temperature, and beat with wooden spoon until dough starts to come away from sides of bowl. Turn onto lightly floured board or tabletop, cover with bowl, and let rest 10 minutes. Knead well to develop elasticity. Kneading should be about 10–15 minutes, or until smooth, adding flour as needed for slightly sticky soft dough.

Form smooth ball, pinching out gas bubbles and creases. Place dough in lightly oiled bowl, turning oiled side up. Cover with damp cloth and let rise in warm place (70°–80°) free from drafts about 1½ hours or until double or triple in bulk. Punch dough down with fist. Let rise again until double or triple in bulk, about 1 hour.

Turn out onto board and punch dough down again. With sharp knife divide dough into 3 equal pieces. After cutting, flip each piece of dough over onto itself. Place at other end of board and cover.

Place each piece in turn onto lightly floured bread board or pastry cloth and roll into a rectangle 8 × 16 inches. Form each piece into very thin loaf approximately 16 inches long, which the French call a *batard*. This is done by rolling dough up jelly roll-fashion. Seal edges by pinching together and then smoothing. Roll loaf back and forth on board to firm, taper, and lengthen as necessary.

Place loaves 3 inches apart on oiled baking sheet sprinkled with cornmeal. Loaves will be very thin but will expand a great deal.

Brush loaves lightly with 1 beaten egg white mixed with 1 Tbsp water or white wine. (This is first step in forming glaze.) Cover loaves with damp cloth tent-like so that towel does not touch loaves (see page 48).

Let rise 1 hour or until double in bulk. With razor or sharp knife gently make 3 diagonal slashes on top of each loaf about $\frac{1}{4}$ inch deep, or slash from end to end.

Preheat oven to 400°. Place pan of boiling water on lower rack of oven. Brush loaves again lightly with egg white mixture and place in oven, reducing heat to 375°.

After 20 minutes quickly brush loaves again with egg white mixture and continue baking until golden brown or until loaves sound hollow when rapped with knuckle (about 40–50 minutes).

Cool bread on rack or place upright in basket, allowing air to circulate.

# POTATO STARTER

(Avoid metal containers and metal spoons with this starter.)

|     |                                            |
| --- | ------------------------------------------ |
| 1   | cup water, body temperature                |
| 1   | tsp honey or sugar                         |
| $\frac{1}{2}$ | tsp salt                         |
| $1\frac{1}{2}$ | cups unbleached white or whole wheat flour |
| 1   | potato, washed, peeled, and grated         |

Into wide-mouthed 1-quart glass container (quart glass measuring cup is handy) put 1 cup water, body temperature, 1 tsp honey or sugar, ½ tsp salt, 1½ cups flour, and enough grated potato to bring mixture to 2-cup level, and mix with wooden spoon.

Leave open or cover with single thickness of cheesecloth (you want to keep out insects but let yeast from air fall in freely). Leave in moderately warm place (75°–85°) for 24 hours. Don't be alarmed if it has strong unpleasant odor and develops dark streaks from potato.

Stir mixture and cover with plastic wrap secured with rubber band. Keep it at same warm temperature for several days, stirring from time to time, until it becomes foamy, rises to 3-cup level (or higher), and begins to have pleasant, yeasty, fermented smell—this may take as long as 1 week.

Stir again, transfer to quart or larger glass jar with tight top, and store in refrigerator until ¼–½ inch of clear liquid rises to top, and bottom of starter is white or cream color. Stir or shake jar every day or so and use at least once a week. If unused for more than a week, stir in 1 tsp sugar on seventh or eighth day to hold it for another week.

To use, take out 1 cup starter, let come to room temperature, and mix into recipe as directed.

After removing 1 cup starter, add ¾ cup flour and ¾ cup water, stir well with wooden spoon, cover tightly, and return to refrigerator.

# AMERICAN SOURDOUGH BREAD

*Makes 2 loaves.* This bread is best if eaten the same day it is baked, or, if tightly wrapped, the next day. Has a fragrance reminiscent of country air, farmhouses, and walking in the woods.

|        |                                          |
|-------:|------------------------------------------|
| 1      | cup potato starter, warmed to room temperature |
| 1½     | cups water, body temperature             |
| 1      | Tbsp light brown sugar                   |
| 1      | Tbsp or pkg dry yeast                    |
| 3½–5½  | cups sifted unbleached white flour       |
| ¼      | cup soy flour                            |
| ¼      | cup wheat germ                           |
| 1      | Tbsp salt                                |
| ½      | tsp baking soda                          |
|        | Cornmeal                                 |
|        | *Glaze:* 1 tsp salt dissolved in 1 cup cold water |

In large mixing bowl pour 1 cup potato starter, warmed to room temperature, 1½ cups water, body temperature, 1 Tbsp brown sugar with lumps broken up, and 1 Tbsp or pkg dry yeast. Stir with wooden spoon until yeast is dissolved.

Add 2½ cups white flour, ¼ cup soy flour, and ¼ cup wheat germ. Beat 4–5 minutes. Cover with plastic or thick towel and set in warm place (75°) free from drafts for 1–2 hours, until light and risen, to make sponge.

Combine 1 Tbsp salt and ½ tsp baking soda with 1 cup flour and stir into sponge. Add additional flour if necessary, until dough forms into ball and comes away from sides of bowl.

Turn out onto floured board and knead, adding more flour as required, until dough is smooth and firm. Cut dough into 2 pieces with sharp knife and shape into 2 loaves.

Place loaves on lightly greased baking sheet, sprinkled with cornmeal. Cover with plastic tent (see directions, page 48), tucking ends under baking sheet to preserve moisture of loaves. Let rise, as patiently as possible, until more than double in bulk (1½–2½ hours). It is very important to let this bread rise sufficiently to get best flavor and texture.

Preheat oven to 425° and put pan of boiling water on bottom rack of oven.

Brush or spray tops of loaves with cold salted water, then slash with very sharp knife, either diagonally several times or from end to end, about ¼–½ inch deep.

Put in oven, turn oven down to 400°, and bake 45 minutes. Brush or spray with salt water again, and return to oven for few minutes more, until crust is as dark as desired. Take from oven and cool on racks.

# Rye Breads

Most rye breads are made with a combination of rye and wheat flours. Because the gluten content of rye flour is so low, wheatless rye breads have a hard time rising. (We have included a wheat-free rye for those allergic to wheat products.)

To give your rye breads as much help rising as possible:

1. Don't sift the rye flour. Unless you use a lot of wheat flour, your rye breads will be heavier and coarser than wheat breads.

2. Warm your rye flour and mixing bowl slightly before starting the bread.

3. Try to provide humid warmth, best for rye risings. A good choice for the "warm place" is an unheated oven—put your covered dough on one rack, with a big panful of warm water on the rack below. (*Note:* If yours is a gas stove with a pilot light in the oven, make sure the oven is not *too* hot. The point of using oven for raising bread is the closed space and the moist warmth of the pan of water—not pilot-flame heat. You can test heat produced by pilot flame with your room thermometer.)

4. Allow a full final rise. Diana's husband, Oscar, has been known to blow it by sticking rye breads in a hot oven for the last rising.

5. To increase humidity during baking, put a pan of hot water in the oven along with your rye.

*Note:* Crackle Glaze (see page 57) is good on rye breads and can be used as an alternative to the glazes given in the recipes below.

# BAKER'S RYE

*Makes 2 loaves.* Bread has a haunting mellow taste. Try mixing in about a cup of raisins for a slightly different flavor.

|       |                                              |
|-------|----------------------------------------------|
| 1     | square or ounce unsweetened chocolate        |
| ½     | cup molasses                                 |
| 1     | Tbsp salt                                    |
| 2     | cups water                                   |
| 2     | Tbsp or pkgs dry yeast                       |
| 1     | cup water, body temperature                  |
| 3     | cups rye flour                               |
| ¼     | cup soy flour                                |
| ¼     | cup wheat germ                               |
| 4½    | cups sifted unbleached white flour           |
| 2     | Tbsp caraway seeds                           |
|       | *Glaze:* 1 tsp instant coffee and 2 Tbsp water; |
|       | or Cornstarch Glaze (see page 56)            |

In saucepan melt 1 square or ounce chocolate. Add ½ cup molasses, 1 Tbsp salt, and 2 cups water. Stir and let mixture cool to body temperature.

In large mixing bowl stir 2 Tbsp or pkgs dry yeast into 1 cup water, body temperature. Set aside.

In medium-size bowl combine and mix 3 cups rye flour, ¼ cup soy flour, ¼ cup wheat germ, 4 cups white flour, and 2 Tbsp caraway seeds.

When chocolate-molasses mixture has cooled sufficiently, stir into yeast in large bowl. Add combined flour, 1 cupful at a time, and beat and knead until well blended. If dough is very sticky add more flour. Turn dough out onto floured board and let rest while you wash, dry, and oil bowl.

Knead dough until smooth, springy, and elastic, adding more flour if dough is still very sticky. Round up into ball and place in oiled bowl, turning dough until well greased.

Cover and set in warm place (75°) free from drafts and let rise until double in bulk (about 1½ hours).

Punch dough down and turn out onto board. Knead 6 times, cut dough in half and shape into long or round loaves. Place in greased pie plates or on baking sheet. Slash tops about ½ inch deep. Let rise until double in bulk (about 1 hour) and bake in preheated 375° oven. Bake 1¼–1¾ hours.

Glaze before putting bread in oven with 1 tsp instant coffee dissolved in 2 Tbsp water, or glaze when removing bread from oven with Cornstarch Glaze.

Remove from pans and cool on racks.

## BLACK BREAD

*Makes 2 loaves.* Aromatic highly flavored black rye bread has an agreeable lingering aftertaste.

|  | |
|---|---|
| 2½ | cups water |
| 4 | Tbsp molasses or honey |
| 4 | Tbsp butter |
| 4 | Tbsp vinegar |
| 1 | square or ounce unsweetened chocolate |
| 1 | Tbsp salt |
| 1 | Tbsp brown sugar |
| 2½–3 | cups unsifted unbleached white flour |
| 4 | cups rye flour |
| 1 | cup bran (if available) |
| 1 | cup wheat germ (if bran is not available use 2 cups wheat germ) |
| 1 | Tbsp whole caraway seeds |
| 1 | tsp fennel seeds, whole or crushed |
| 2 | Tbsp or pkgs dry yeast |
| 1 | Tbsp instant coffee |
|  | Cornmeal |
|  | *Glaze:* Cornstarch Glaze (see page 56) |

In saucepan heat to lukewarm 2½ cups water, 4 Tbsp molasses or honey, 4 Tbsp butter, 4 Tbsp vinegar, 1 square or ounce unsweetened chocolate, 1 Tbsp salt, and 1 Tbsp brown sugar. When butter and chocolate have almost melted, set aside to cool to body temperature.

In very large bowl combine 2½ cups white flour, 4 cups rye flour, 1 cup bran, 1 cup wheat germ, 1 Tbsp whole caraway seeds, 1 tsp fennel seeds, 2 Tbsp or pkgs dry yeast, and 1 Tbsp instant coffee. Stir cooled liquid mixture into dry ingredients and mix well. Dough will be stiff and rather moist. Turn out onto well-floured board and cover with bowl for about 15 minutes, allowing dough to rest. Now knead dough until smooth and elastic, about 15 minutes, adding more flour if needed.

Place in greased bowl, turning dough so that it is well greased, cover, and set in a warm place (75°–80°) free from drafts. This dough takes a while to rise. To hurry it along you can place bowl in larger container half filled with warm water and cover both containers. (This is even quicker than putting dough in oven with pan of warm water.) Handled this way, dough will take 1–2 hours for first rising. It may not quite double in bulk.

Punch dough down and divide into 2 portions. Shape each half either into ball or oblong loaf. Place in soufflé dish or pie plate, or on baking sheet, greased and dusted with cornmeal. Cover and let rise again until about double in bulk, about 1–2 hours. (Let dough rise as much as it will because it will stop immediately when placed in preheated oven.)

Preheat oven to 350° and bake until done or about 1 hour. Ten minutes before bread is ready to come out of the oven glaze with Cornstarch Glaze. Return bread to oven and bake 10 minutes more until glaze is set. Cool on a rack.

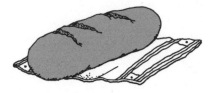

*Yeast Breads*

# BEST SOFT PUMPERNICKEL

*Makes 2 loaves.* Moist, soft, sweet, and compelling, this is a bread to satisfy deep hunger, or stimulate the appetite.

| | |
|---|---|
| 3 | Tbsp or pkgs dry yeast |
| 1½ | cups water, body temperature |
| ½ | cup brewed strong coffee, cooled to body temperature |
| ½ | cup honey |
| ¼ | cup molasses |
| 2 | Tbsp softened butter |
| 4½ | cups unsifted unbleached white flour |
| 1½ | cups whole wheat flour |
| 2 | cups rye flour (plus extra rye flour for kneading in) |
| 4 | tsp salt |
| | Cornmeal |
| | *Glaze:* 1 Tbsp melted butter or 1 egg white mixed with 2 Tbsp water or Cornstarch Glaze (see page 56) |

In large bowl sprinkle 3 Tbsp or pkgs dry yeast in a mixture of 1½ cups water and ½ cup strong brewed coffee, both body temperature. Stir and set aside for 5 minutes. Now stir in ½ cup honey, ¼ cup molasses, and 2 Tbsp softened butter.

In another bowl blend 4½ cups white flour, 1½ cups whole wheat flour, 2 cups rye flour, and 4 tsp salt. Slowly add this blend to liquids, stirring until dough comes away from sides of bowl, adding more rye flour if necessary.

Lightly flour board or table with rye flour. Knead dough until smooth, about 5–7 minutes, adding more rye flour to make firm dough.

Place dough in greased bowl and turn over so greased side is up. Cover with towel and let rise in warm place (75°–80°) free from drafts until double in bulk (about 1½–2½ hours).

---

Punch dough down. Divide in half and form into balls. Place each ball, smooth side up, in pie plate or on baking sheet that has been greased and sprinkled with cornmeal. Cover with towel and let rise for 1 hour, or until double in bulk.

Preheat oven to 450°.

For soft crust brush with melted butter before putting bread in oven. For firmer, shinier crust, brush loaves with egg white mixed with 2 Tbsp water. Or use Cornstarch Glaze 10 minutes before loaves are ready to come out of oven.

Bake breads at 450° for 10 minutes. Lower heat to 350° and continue to bake for an additional 50 minutes. Rap bread with your knuckle to test if it is hollow and done.

Remove from pans or sheet and cool on wire racks.


## DARK RYE BREAD

*Makes 2 loaves.* This is a delicately textured, good, serviceable rye.

|       |                                      |
|-------|--------------------------------------|
| 2     | cups water, body temperature         |
| 2     | Tbsp or pkgs dry yeast               |
| 1/4   | cup soy flour                        |
| 3     | cups rye flour                       |
| 3     | cups sifted unbleached white flour   |
| 1     | Tbsp salt                            |
| 1/4   | cup molasses                         |
| 2     | Tbsp soft butter                     |
| 1     | Tbsp caraway seeds (optional)        |
|       | Cornmeal                             |
|       | *Glaze:* 1 egg white mixed with 1 Tbsp water |

In large bowl place 2 cups water, body temperature, and 2 Tbsp or pkgs dry yeast. Stir and set aside.

In another bowl mix thoroughly ¼ cup soy flour, 3 cups rye flour, and 3 cups white flour.

To yeast mixture add 1 Tbsp salt, ¼ cup molasses, 2 Tbsp soft butter, and 1 Tbsp caraway seeds, if you like them. Add half of flour mixture, beating until smooth. Gradually add remaining flour 1 cup at a time, beating with wooden spoon until dough starts to leave sides of bowl. Turn out onto floured bread board or tabletop. Cover dough and let rest while you wash, dry, and grease bowl.

Knead until dough is smooth and firm. Form dough into ball and place in greased bowl, turning until dough is evenly greased. Cover and put in warm place (70°–80°) free from drafts. Dough will double in bulk in about 1 hour.

Punch down and turn out on board. With sharp knife, cut dough in half and either form into 2 balls to make round loaves or shape into long 12-inch loaves, using jelly roll method. Place loaves on baking sheet, greased and dusted with cornmeal. Cover with towel and let rise second time until double in bulk.

Preheat oven to 375°.

Glaze bread by brushing with 1 slightly beaten egg white mixed with 1 Tbsp water and sprinkle with 1 Tbsp caraway seeds (optional).

Bake bread about 1 hour or until bread sounds hollow when thumped. Remove from baking sheet and cool on racks.

# JUST-RYE BREAD

*Makes 2 medium loaves.* A very good bread for those who love rye best or who are allergic to wheat products. The crust is chewy but the texture is very soft and spongy. Bread is also good saltless.

| | |
|---|---|
| 1 | Tbsp or pkg dry yeast |
| ¾ | cup water, body temperature |
| 1 | cup brewed tea, body temperature |
| ½ | cup molasses |
| ¼ | cup melted butter, cooled |
| 1 | cup mashed potatoes, room temperature |
| 3 | eggs, separated |
| 2 | tsp salt (optional) |
| 7–7½ | cups rye flour |
| | Cornmeal |
| | *Glaze:* 1 Tbsp melted butter followed by |
| | Cornstarch Glaze (see page 56) |

In small bowl stir 1 Tbsp yeast into ¾ cup water, body temperature. Set aside.

In large mixing bowl combine 1 cup brewed tea, body temperature, ½ cup molasses, and ¼ cup melted cooled butter.

In separate container blend 1 cup mashed potatoes, room temperature, and 3 egg yolks. Add to ingredients in large bowl. Add yeast mixture and stir until liquid and smooth.

With rotary beater whip 3 egg whites until stiff. Fold into liquid ingredients. If you desire salt, add 2 tsp salt to 5 cups flour. Add rye flour to liquid ingredients 1 cup at a time until dough starts to come away from sides of bowl. Turn dough out onto rye-floured board and knead in additional flour until fairly stiff. Cover dough with bowl and let rest 20–30 minutes.

Divide dough in half and form loaves; place them in greased medium-size bread pans or put them on baking sheet, greased and sprinkled with cornmeal. Brush with butter and cover tent-like so that plastic or cloth does not touch dough (see page 48). Let rise in warm place (75°–80°) until dough reaches top of bread pan or doubles in bulk. (This may take several hours, as rye dough sometimes rises *very* slowly.)

Preheat oven to 375°. Put in loaves, turn down to 350° and bake about 1 hour or more, or until loaves sound hollow when thumped. Loaves will come out rye color (gray). We recommend reglazing with Cornstarch Glaze and returning loaves to oven for about 10 minutes at 325°. Cool on racks.


## ✓   ANISE-RAISIN RYE

*Makes 2 loaves.* Good plain or spread with cream cheese for lunch or tea.

|        |                                              |
|--------|----------------------------------------------|
| 2      | Tbsp or pkgs dry yeast                       |
| 2½     | cups water, body temperature                 |
| ¼      | cup molasses                                 |
| ¼      | cup melted butter or oil                     |
| 4      | cups rye flour                               |
| 3½–4   | cups sifted unbleached white flour           |
| ¼      | cup soy flour                                |
| ¼      | cup wheat germ                               |
| ½      | cup nonfat dry milk                          |
| 1      | Tbsp salt                                    |
| 2      | Tbsp instant coffee powder                   |
| 2      | Tbsp dried orange peel                       |
| 1–1½   | Tbsp anise seeds                             |
|        | (whole or crushed in mortar)                 |
| 1–1½   | cups raisins                                 |
|        | Cornmeal                                     |
|        | *Glaze:* 1 egg white mixed with 1 Tbsp       |
|        | cold water                                   |

In small container sprinkle 2 Tbsp or pkgs yeast over ½ cup water, body temperature. Stir and set aside.

In medium-size bowl blend 2 cups water, body temperature, ¼ cup molasses, and ¼ cup melted butter or oil.

In very large bowl combine and mix well, 4 cups rye flour, 3 cups white flour, ¼ cup soy flour, ¼ cup wheat germ, ½ cup nonfat dry milk, 1 Tbsp salt, 2 Tbsp instant coffee powder, 2 Tbsp dried orange peel, 1–1½ Tbsp anise seeds, and 1–1½ cups raisins.

When flours are well mixed pour in yeast mixture and liquids. Beat with wooden spoon and then knead, adding as much as 1 additional cup of white flour if necessary to make very stiff dough. Let dough rest for 20 minutes covered with bowl.

Wash, dry, and grease bowl. Knead dough a few more times, round up into a ball and place in bowl, turning so that ball is well greased. Cover and let dough rise in warm place (75°–80°) free from drafts until double in bulk, about 5–6 hours. (Try setting bowl in unheated oven with large pan of warm water on rack below.)

Turn out dough and knead a few times. Divide in half and form 2 round or oblong loaves. Place on baking sheet, greased and dusted with cornmeal, cover with plastic, and let rise until double. (We frequently leave it out overnight and bake loaves in the morning.)

Preheat oven to 375°. Glaze loaves with beaten egg white mixed with 1 Tbsp cold water. Place in oven and bake for 1 hour or until loaves sound hollow when thumped. Cool on racks.

# LIMPA BREAD WITH BEER

*Makes 2 medium loaves.* If you want an occasional stimulating change from other ryes, bake this tasty, highly flavored rye bread.

| | |
|---:|:---|
| ½ | cup water, body temperature |
| 2 | Tbsp or pkgs dry yeast |
| 1¼ | cups beer, warmed to body temperature |
| ¼ | cup dark brown sugar |
| ¼ | cup molasses |
| 3 | Tbsp oil |
| ½ | tsp anise seed, whole or crushed in a mortar |
| 3 | cups sifted unbleached white flour |
| ¼ | cup wheat germ |
| ¼ | cup soy flour |
| 2–2½ | cups rye flour |
| 1 | Tbsp salt |
| 2 | Tbsp dried orange peel |
| | Cornmeal |
| | *Glaze:* Cornstarch Glaze (see page 56) |

Into ½ cup water, body temperature, stir 2 Tbsp or pkgs dry yeast, and set aside.

Warm 1¼ cups beer in pan to body temperature or a little higher, turn off heat and mix in ¼ cup dark brown sugar with lumps broken up, ¼ cup molasses, and 3 Tbsp oil.

In large mixing bowl mix ½ tsp anise seed, whole or crushed, 3 cups white flour, ¼ cup wheat germ, and ¼ cup soy flour. Add liquid ingredients and yeast mixture and beat for 5 minutes.

Cover and let rise in warm place (75°–80°) until light and bubbly (up to 1 hour).

Stir down, then stir in 2 cups rye flour, 1 Tbsp salt, and 2 Tbsp dried orange peel.

Turn onto board or counter floured with rye flour and knead, adding enough rye flour to make firm and elastic dough that does not stick to kneading surface or hands.

Wash, dry, and oil bowl. Round dough up and return dough to bowl, turning dough until ball is lightly coated with oil. Cover and let rise second time in warm place (75°–80°) until double in bulk (1 hour or more).

Punch dough down, turn out, and knead a few times. Cut dough in half with sharp knife and form round loaves.

Place loaves on lightly oiled baking sheet sprinkled with cornmeal, and cover, tent-like, with cloth or plastic, so cover does not touch loaves (see page 48). Set in warm place (75°–80°) until loaves double in bulk third time.

Heat oven to 375°, carefully slash loaves with very sharp knife or razor ½ inch deep both ways, making an "X". Bake about 1 hour, or until loaves sound hollow when rapped with knuckle.

If you like a hard crust, after 50 minutes of baking, glaze loaves with Cornstarch Glaze, and return to oven for 10 minutes more.

Remove loaves from oven and cool on wire racks.

# GOLDEN BROWN SOUR RYE

*Makes 2 loaves.* Allow plenty of time for this deliciously sour 80 percent rye bread. Beware of inhaling the enticing aroma of the sour mixture too long or you may become a little drunk.

6–6½    cups unsifted rye flour (your own coarsely
           home-ground rye meal is delicious to use,
           if available)
    1    cup sifted unbleached white flour
    1    Tbsp or pkg dry yeast (or 2 homemade
           yeast cakes, nice in this bread)
   ⅓    cup molasses or malt syrup
  2½    cups water, body temperature
    1    Tbsp salt
        Cornmeal
        *Glaze:* Cornstarch Glaze (optional—see page 56)

The night before, place in large mixing bowl 1½ cups rye flour, 1 cup white flour, 1 Tbsp or pkg dry yeast (or 2 home-made yeast cakes, crumbled), and ⅓ cup molasses or malt syrup. Add 2½ cups water, body temperature, and stir until all lumps are dissolved and blended. (Wire whisk is good.) Leave in warm place (75°–80°) such as in unheated oven with pan of warm water beneath it, covered with cheesecloth or very light towel, until sour or until next day. (Souring, if left uncovered, takes about 6–8 hours.)

When mixture is sour or next day, add 1 Tbsp salt and 4½ cups or more rye flour to mixture, reserving ½ cup to blend in on board while kneading. (Bread will probably not take all additional flour.) Knead until firm. Form into 2 balls or oblong loaves, place on baking sheet, greased and dusted with corn-meal, cover, and let rise in warm place (75°–80°) free from drafts until double in bulk. This will take several hours.

Bake in preheated 325° oven for about 1½ hours or until

done when tested. Glazing loaves with Cornstarch Glaze brings out golden color of rye. Remove from oven and cool on racks.

## CHEWY SOUR RYE BREAD

*Makes 2 large loaves.* Very chewy bread flavored with the very essence of rye.

*Note:* Read through entire recipe before starting. Make sure you have on hand at least 6 cups rye flour, 2 cups white flour, molasses, caraway seeds, cornmeal, cornstarch, salt, and yeast.

The day before you want to bake this bread, prepare the following:

*Sour Mixture*
1   Tbsp or pkg dry yeast (or 2 homemade yeast cakes)
1   cup water, body temperature
2   cups rye flour

In medium-size bowl stir 1 Tbsp or pkg dry yeast (or 2 homemade yeast cakes, crumbled) into 1 cup water, body temperature. Stir in 2 cups rye flour, cover, and let stand in warm place (70°–80°) for 24 hours until sour.
Twenty-four hours later, when mixture is sufficiently sour, stir down. Set aside.

In large bowl prepare "sponge" as follows:

*Sponge Mixture*
1   Tbsp or pkg dry yeast
1   cup water, body temperature
2   cups unsifted unbleached white flour
1   cup rye flour

In large bowl stir 1 Tbsp or pkg dry yeast into 1 cup water, body temperature. In third bowl combine 2 cups white flour and 1 cup rye flour. Mix in with yeast and water in large bowl.

Add *sour* mixture to *sponge* mixture and mix as well as possible with wooden spoon about 10 minutes or longer. (Mixture will be very stiff and sticky.) Cover and let rise in warm place (70°–80°) about 2 hours.

Now you are ready to make actual dough.

    3    cups rye flour
    1½   Tbsp salt
    1–2  Tbsp caraway seeds, ground or whole, to taste
    2    Tbsp molasses
    1    cup water, body temperature
         Cornmeal
         *Glaze:* Cornstarch Glaze (see page 56)

Mix 3 cups rye flour, 1½ Tbsp salt and 1–2 Tbsp caraway seeds together in second large bowl. Dilute 2 Tbsp molasses in 1 cup water, body temperature, and mix with flour mixture. Combine this with "sour-sponge" preparation and beat and knead until completely incorporated. Dough will probably still be sticky and stiff. Try rubbing a little oil on board and hands to keep dough from sticking quite as much. Let dough rest 15 minutes.

Form into 2 balls or oblong loaves. Place in large greased loaf pans, soufflé dishes, or on greased baking sheet dusted lightly with cornmeal. Let rise 30–45 minutes and bake in preheated 375° oven for 1 hour or until bread sounds hollow when rapped with knuckle.

Ten minutes before loaves are ready to come out of oven brush with Cornstarch Glaze and return to oven for 10 minutes for glaze to harden. This will make a nice hard crust. Remove from oven and cool on racks.

# Variety Breads

# FINE-TEXTURED OATMEAL BREAD

*Makes 2 medium loaves.* Bread has a fine delicate texture and is delicious. Dough can also be made into rolls—about 3 dozen.

|  |  |
|---:|:---|
| 1 | Tbsp or pkg dry yeast |
| ⅔ | cup water, body temperature |
| 1 | cup milk, scalded and cooled |
|  | to body temperature |
| Scant ½ | cup light brown sugar |
| 1 | Tbsp salt |
| ½ | cup butter |
| 4–5 | cups unsifted unbleached white flour |
| ¼ | cup wheat germ |
| ¼ | cup soy flour |
| 2 | eggs, lightly beaten |
| 1⅓ | cups rolled oats |

In large bowl sprinkle 1 Tbsp or pkg dry yeast over ⅔ cup water, body temperature, and stir. Set aside.

After scalding 1 cup milk in saucepan, add scant ½ cup light brown sugar, 1 Tbsp salt, and ½ cup butter, stirring to dissolve. Set aside to cool to body temperature.

Combine 4 cups white flour, ¼ cup wheat germ, and ¼ cup soy flour, mixing well.

When milk solution has cooled sufficiently, add to dissolved yeast in large bowl. Stir in 2 lightly beaten eggs and 1⅓ cups rolled oats.

Gradually add dry ingredients to liquid, stirring, beating, and kneading until dough starts to leave sides of bowl. Turn dough out onto board. Knead about 10 minutes, adding additional flour to make soft, smooth, elastic dough. Form into ball.

Let dough rest while you wash, dry, and oil bowl. Place dough in oiled bowl, turning to coat evenly with oil. Cover dough and let rise in warm place (70°–80°) free from drafts until double in bulk, about 1 hour.

Punch dough down in bowl, turn out on lightly floured board, cover with bowl, and let rest 10 minutes. Cut dough in half and shape into 2 loaves. Place in greased medium-size bread pans. Cover pans with plastic or towel and let rise in warm place (70°–80°) until double, about 45 minutes.

Preheat oven to 375° and bake loaves for 45 minutes to 1 hour or until bread sounds hollow when thumped. Remove from pans and cool on racks.

## POTATO BREAD

*Makes 2 large loaves.* This chewy bread is very similar in appearance to white bread but tastes rather different. Delicious toasted and plain. Very good way to use leftover mashed potato.

| | |
|---|---|
| 1 | medium-size potato, or about ⅔ cup mashed potato |
| 1 | cup plain water or potato water, body temperature |
| 2 | Tbsp or pkgs dry yeast |
| 1 | cup scalded milk, cooled to a little warmer than body temperature |
| 3 | Tbsp butter |
| ¼ | cup soy flour |
| ¼ | cup wheat germ |
| 6¼–6¾ | cups sifted unbleached white flour |
| 2 | Tbsp light brown sugar |
| 1 | Tbsp salt |
| | *Glaze:* 1 Tbsp melted butter (optional) |

*If you are starting with a raw potato,* wash, pare, and cut into quarters. Boil in water until tender. Remove from water and mash. Set aside. Add enough additional water to potato water to make 1 cup. Set aside to cool to body temperature. When sufficiently cooled pour into large bowl and sprinkle 2 Tbsp or pkgs dry yeast over water. Stir and set aside.

*If you are using leftover mashed potato* which has been stored in the refrigerator, measure ⅔ cup and let it stand long enough to reach room temperature. Pour 1 cup water, body temperature, into large bowl and sprinkle 2 Tbsp or pkgs dry yeast over water. Stir and set aside.

In saucepan scald 1 cup milk. Add 3 Tbsp butter to hot milk and let mixture cool to a little warmer than body temperature.

In medium-size bowl combine ¼ cup soy flour, ¼ cup wheat germ, 6 cups white flour, 2 Tbsp brown sugar with lumps broken up, and 1 Tbsp salt.

Mix mashed potato into milk-butter mixture. Add to yeast and water in large bowl. Stir. Beat flour mixture into liquids in large bowl 1 cup at a time. When dough starts to form into ball, knead in bowl a few minutes and then turn out onto floured board and continue kneading until dough is smooth and elastic. Knead in additional flour as needed to make fairly stiff dough. Wash, dry, and oil bowl. Round dough up and return to greased bowl, turning until dough is greased. Cover. Set in warm place (70°–80°) free from drafts and let rise until double (about 45 minutes to 1 hour).

Punch dough down, round up, cover, and let rise second time (about 1 hour).

Punch dough down, turn out onto board, knead a few times and divide dough in half. Form into loaves. Place in greased large bread pans. Cover and let rise third time in warm place (70°–80°) free from drafts until double in bulk (about 1 hour).

Either dust tops with flour or glaze with melted butter and bake in preheated 375° oven for about 45 minutes to 1 hour, or until bread sounds hollow when thumped. Remove from pans and cool on wire rack.

# SALTLESS WHEAT GERM BREAD

*Makes 1 medium loaf.* This light, likable loaf has an agreeable blandness.

|       |                                      |
|-------|--------------------------------------|
| 1     | Tbsp or pkg dry yeast                |
| ½     | tsp sugar                            |
| 1     | cup water, body temperature          |
| 2     | Tbsp honey                           |
| 1½    | Tbsp melted butter or oil            |
| ¼     | cup soy flour                        |
| ⅓     | cup nonfat dry milk                  |
| 1     | cup wheat germ                       |
| 2–2¼  | cups sifted unbleached white flour   |
|       | *Glaze:* 1 Tbsp melted butter (optional) |

In small container sprinkle 1 Tbsp or pkg dry yeast and ½ tsp sugar over ¼ cup water, body temperature. Stir and set aside in warm place until bubbling.

Combine in bowl 2 Tbsp honey and 1½ Tbsp melted butter or oil with ¾ cup water, body temperature, and stir until dissolved. Set aside.

In medium-size bowl mix ¼ cup soy flour, ⅓ cup nonfat dry milk, 1 cup wheat germ, and 1 cup white flour. Stir until well blended.

Combine all liquid ingredients and pour all at once into dry ingredients. Beat and knead until dough forms ball and starts to separate from sides of bowl. Turn out onto lightly floured board and continue kneading in more white flour until dough is smooth and just a little sticky. Wash, dry, and grease bowl. Round up dough and return to bowl, turning greased side up. Cover and let rise in warm place (70°–80°) free from drafts until double in bulk (about 1½ hours). Punch dough down and form into loaf. Place in greased medium-size pan. Brush top with melted butter (optional) and let rise until double or until dough reaches top of bread pan, about 1½ hours. No more rising will occur in oven. Bake in preheated 350° oven for about 40 minutes to 1 hour, or until done. Remove from pan and cool on rack.

## ONION LOAF

*Makes 2 large loaves or 1 large loaf and 4 mini loaves.* The delicately onion-flavored taste of this bread can be increased or decreased as you like.

|       |                                                |
|------:|------------------------------------------------|
| 2     | cups milk, scalded and cooled<br>to body temperature |
| 2     | Tbsp butter                                    |
| 2     | Tbsp brown sugar or molasses                   |
| 1     | Tbsp salt                                      |
| 2     | Tbsp or pkgs dry yeast                         |
| ½     | cup water, body temperature                    |
| 2½–3  | cups sifted unbleached white flour             |
| ½     | cup soy flour                                  |
| 3     | cups whole wheat flour                         |
| ½     | tsp celery seeds                               |
| ¼     | cup dried onion or 1 cup diced fresh onion     |
|       | *Glaze:* 1 egg yolk and 2 Tbsp water           |

In saucepan scald 2 cups milk. Add 2 Tbsp butter, 2 Tbsp brown sugar or molasses and 1 Tbsp salt. Stir to dissolve and set aside to cool to body temperature.

---

In small bowl stir 2 Tbsp or pkgs dry yeast into ½ cup water, body temperature. Set aside.

Using large mixing bowl combine 2½ cups white flour, ½ cup soy flour, 3 cups whole wheat flour, and ½ tsp celery seeds.

Dice about 1 cup fresh onion or use ¼ cup dried onion. Add to flour mixture and stir to coat onions with flour before adding liquid. (Reserve 1–2 tsp onion for crust, if you like.)

Make a well in flour and pour in yeast mixture. Add cooled milk mixture and beat and knead dough until well blended. When dough starts to leave sides of bowl, turn out onto board and knead about 10 minutes until dough is smooth, elastic, and stiff, adding more white flour as needed to gain this consistency.

Round dough up and place in greased bowl, turning greased side up. Let rise, covered, in warm place (70°–80°) free from drafts until double in bulk (about 1–2 hours).

Turn dough out onto board and punch down. Cover and let rest for 10–15 minutes. Form dough into ball and cut in half. Shape 2 large loaves or 1 large and 4 mini loaves. Put in greased bread pans and let rise until 1 inch from top of pan or double in bulk (about 1 hour). Glaze with egg yolk and 2 Tbsp water. Sprinkle on reserved onion, if you wish.

Bake in preheated 400° oven for 50–60 minutes or until done. Remove from pans and cool on rack.

# RAISIN CINNAMON SPIRAL LOAF

*Makes 2 medium loaves or 1 medium loaf and 4 mini loaves.*
Children of all ages love this delicious bread. Great plain, with
butter, cream cheese, toasted or any way you like.

| | |
|---|---|
| 1½ | cups milk, scalded and cooled to body temperature |
| ½ | cup butter |
| 2 | Tbsp or pkgs dry yeast |
| ½ | cup water, body temperature |
| ¼ | cup soy flour |
| ¼ | cup wheat germ |
| 1 | cup whole wheat flour |
| About 6 | cups sifted unbleached white flour |
| ¼ | cup light brown sugar |
| 1 | Tbsp salt |
| 1½ | cups raisins, yellow or black |
| 3 | eggs, slightly beaten |
| ½ | cup chopped nuts (your choice, though walnuts are good) |
| ¾ | cup sugar |
| 1 | Tbsp cinnamon |
| | *Glaze:* ¼ cup melted butter |

In saucepan scald 1½ cups milk, add ½ cup butter, and
set aside to cool to body temperature.

In large bowl sprinkle 2 Tbsp or pkgs dry yeast over ½ cup
water, body temperature. Stir and set aside.

In medium-size bowl combine ¼ cup soy flour, ¼ cup wheat
germ, 1 cup whole wheat flour, 3 cups white flour, ¼ cup brown
sugar with lumps broken up, 1 Tbsp salt, and 1½ cups raisins,
yellow or black.

Combine cooled scalded milk and butter with 3 slightly
beaten eggs and pour into yeast mixture. Add combined flour
to liquid ingredients and beat until smooth. Add additional

flour, 1 cupful at a time, until dough forms ball and comes away from sides of bowl.

Turn dough out onto lightly floured board and let rest while you wash, dry, and grease bowl. Knead dough until smooth and elastic, about 10–15 minutes. Round dough up and return to greased bowl, turning so that dough is well greased. Cover with towel and let rise in warm place (70°–80°) free from drafts about 1½ hours, or until double in bulk.

Combine ½ cup chopped nuts with ¾ cup sugar and 1 Tbsp cinnamon.

Turn dough out onto lightly floured board and divide dough in half (or cut 1 half of dough into 4 pieces for mini loaves). Roll each piece of dough in turn into long rectangle and sprinkle with sugar-nut mixture. Roll up like jelly roll (see "Shaping," p. 49), pinching seams and ends together to form smooth loaves. Carefully place in buttered medium-size bread pans (or mini pans) and brush tops with melted butter. Cover with towel and let rise until double in bulk or about 1 inch from top of pan, about 1 hour.

Preheat oven to 375°. Brush raised loaves again with melted butter and sprinkle with cinnamon and sugar, if you wish, though it might be too sweet for you.

Bake 35–40 minutes for mini loaves and 1 hour for larger loaves. Loaves are done when they sound hollow when thumped. Remove from pans and cool on wire rack.

*Yeast Breads*

# ✓ RAISIN-PLENTY BREAD

*Makes 2 large loaves.* Delicious cut thick and served with tea or coffee; particularly good for snacks. There are plenty of raisins, which give it added nutritional value.

|        |                                              |
|-------:|----------------------------------------------|
| 2      | cups milk, scalded and cooled to body temperature |
| ½      | cup butter                                   |
| 3      | Tbsp or pkgs dry yeast                        |
| ¼      | cup water, body temperature                   |
| 2      | tsp salt                                      |
| 2      | Tbsp brown sugar                              |
| ¼      | cup wheat germ                                |
| ¼      | cup soy flour                                 |
| 1      | cup whole wheat pastry flour                  |
| About 7| cups sifted unbleached white flour            |
| 2      | cups black raisins                            |
| 3      | eggs, slightly beaten                         |
|        | *Glaze:* 1 Tbsp melted butter                 |

In saucepan scald 2 cups milk. Add ½ cup butter and cool to body temperature.

Sprinkle 3 Tbsp or pkgs dry yeast over ¼ cup water, body temperature. Stir and set aside.

In very large mixing bowl combine 2 tsp salt, 2 Tbsp brown sugar with lumps broken up, ¼ cup wheat germ, ¼ cup soy flour, 1 cup whole wheat flour, and about 5 cups white flour. Stir in 2 cups raisins until they are well coated with flour mixture.

Add 3 slightly beaten eggs to cooled milk-butter mixture. Combine with yeast-water mixture and pour all at once into dry ingredients. With wooden spoon stir and beat until smooth. Add additional flour in ½-cup measures, working into dough until it starts to come away from sides of bowl. Turn dough out onto lightly floured board and knead until smooth and elastic, about 10 minutes. Wash, dry, and grease bowl. Round dough up and return to bowl, turning so that greased side is up. Cover and let rise in warm place (70°–80°) free from drafts until double in bulk, about 1 hour. Punch dough down and divide in half. Shape into loaves and place in greased large bread pans. Cover and let rise second time. Brush with melted butter.

Bake in preheated 400° oven for about 1½ hours or until hollow sounding when thumped. Remove from pans and cool on racks.

## FRAGRANT LIGHT AND DARK BREAD

*Makes 3 medium loaves.* Use your imagination here for shaping—we give you one suggestion. The dough is also excellent for making unusual rolls.

| | |
|---|---|
| 2 | Tbsp or pkgs dry yeast |
| 1 | tsp sugar |
| 2½ | cups water, body temperature |
| ½ | cup molasses |
| 3 | cups sifted unbleached white flour |
| ¾ | cup nonfat dry milk |
| ½ | square or ½ ounce unsweetened chocolate |
| 1 | tsp instant coffee powder |
| ¼ | cup molasses |
| ¼ | cup hot water |
| 4 | Tbsp melted butter |

$\checkmark$

|       |                                       |
|-------|---------------------------------------|
| 1     | Tbsp salt                             |
| 2¾–3  | cups whole wheat flour                |
| ¼     | cup water, body temperature           |
| 3½–3¾ | cups sifted unbleached white flour    |
|       | *Glaze:* 1 Tbsp melted butter and     |
|       | Cornstarch Glaze (see page 56)        |

In small container sprinkle 2 Tbsp or pkgs dry yeast and 1 tsp sugar into ½ cup water, body temperature. Stir and set aside until it starts to bubble (about 10 minutes).

In large bowl combine 2 cups water, body temperature, with ½ cup molasses, 3 cups white flour, and ¾ cup nonfat dry milk. Add bubbling yeast mixture and beat until well mixed.

Cover bowl with plastic and let "sponge" (batter with yeast added) develop overnight in refrigerator. Or cover with towel, set in warm place (70°–80°) and let sponge form (about 2½–3 hours). Proceed when sponge becomes light and airy.

In saucepan melt ½ square unsweetened chocolate, 1 tsp instant coffee powder and ¼ cup molasses in ¼ cup hot water. Cool mixture to body temperature. Set aside.

Add 4 Tbsp melted butter and 1 Tbsp salt to sponge that has formed and beat down vigorously. Divide sponge in half (each half about 2½ cups).

To first half of sponge add chocolate-coffee-molasses mixture. Work in about 2¾–3 cups whole wheat flour. When dough leaves sides of bowl, turn out onto board and knead until smooth and elastic. Form into ball and place in greased bowl, turning until well greased.

To second half of sponge add ¼ cup water, body temperature, and work in about 3½–3¾ cups white flour. Knead until smooth and elastic. Form into ball. Wash, dry, and grease bowl. Place ball of dough in bowl, turning until well greased.

Cover bowls and let rise in warm place (70°–80°) free from drafts until double in bulk ( about 1 hour).

Turn out whole wheat ball of dough and knead lightly, pressing out gas. Divide into 6 pieces. Shape each piece into rope

---

*Yeast Breads*                                          125

slightly longer than bread pan. Repeat with white flour ball.

On board place 1 dark rope beside 1 light rope. Place 1 light rope on top of dark rope. Place 1 dark rope on top of light rope. Twist all 4 ropes several times without intermixing doughs. Put in medium-size loaf pan with ends flat against ends of pan. Repeat procedure with other ropes or devise your own designs.

Glaze tops with butter, cover with towel and let rise until double in bulk. This will take some time, as the whole wheat dough is slower to rise than the white.

Bake in preheated 350° oven for about 1 hour. Ten minutes before loaves are done, remove from pans, brush with Cornstarch Glaze and return loaves to oven for about 6–10 minutes for glaze to set. Remove from oven and cool on wire rack.

## SALT-FREE RICE BREAD

*Makes 1 medium loaf.* You can use either white rice flour or brown rice flour to make this recipe.

- 3 Tbsp brown sugar
- 1 cup water, body temperature
- 1 Tbsp or pkg dry yeast
- 3 Tbsp oil
- 2 cups plus 1 Tbsp unsifted unbleached white flour
- 1 cup white or brown rice flour
- 1 Tbsp melted sweet butter

*Yeast Breads*

In large bowl combine 3 Tbsp brown sugar with the lumps broken up, and 1 cup water, body temperature. Sprinkle in 1 Tbsp or pkg dry yeast. Stir and let stand 5 minutes. Stir in 3 Tbsp oil.

Mix together in another bowl 2 cups plus 1 Tbsp white flour and 1 cup rice flour. Stir, beat, and knead flour into liquid ingredients.

Turn dough out onto floured board and knead dough with floured hands about 3 minutes. Place it in greased bowl. Spread ½ Tbsp melted sweet butter over this dough. Cover with towel and let rise in warm place (70°–80°) free from drafts until double in bulk.

Punch dough down and knead. Shape it into loaf and place it in greased medium-size loaf pan. Spread remaining melted butter on top. Cover with towel and let rise in warm place (70°–80°) until double in bulk.

Bake in preheated 325° oven for 50 minutes to 1 hour or until loaf sounds hollow when tapped.

Remove from pan and cool on wire rack.


## SESAME-HERB BREADSTICKS

*Makes 24 breadsticks.* Crunchy and full of flavor, perfect for snacking.

|  |  |
|---|---|
| 1 | Tbsp or pkg dry yeast |
| 1¼ | cups water, body temperature |
| 3 | Tbsp dark brown sugar |
| 1½ | tsp salt |
| 1 | Tbsp soft butter |
| 1 | Tbsp roasted sesame seeds |
| ½ | tsp ground sage |
| ½ | tsp thyme |
| 3–3¼ | cups sifted unbleached white flour |

Using large bowl, sprinkle 1 Tbsp or pkg dry yeast over 1¼ cups water, body temperature. Add 1 Tbsp dark brown sugar. Stir. Let stand until mixture is bubbly (about 5 minutes).

Stir in remaining 2 Tbsp dark brown sugar, with lumps broken up, 1½ tsp salt, 1 Tbsp soft butter, 1 Tbsp roasted sesame seeds, ½ tsp ground sage, ½ tsp thyme, and 3–3¼ cups white flour. Mix well.

Turn out onto lightly floured board. Knead dough about 10 minutes, until smooth and elastic.

Form dough into smooth ball and place in greased mixing bowl, turning over once to oil dough. Cover with damp cloth and let rise in warm place (70°–80°) free from drafts until double in bulk, about 1 hour.

Punch dough down with fist. Turn onto lightly floured board. Take sharp knife and divide dough in half.

Flatten each half into rectangle about 12 inches long. With sharp knife, divide each rectangle into 12 pieces. Roll each piece into a rope about 11–12 inches long.

Put ropes on greased cookie sheets. Cover and let rise in warm place until double in bulk (about 1 hour).

Preheat oven to 400°. Bake 15–20 minutes or until slightly brown. Cool on racks.

# ZWIEBACK

*Makes about 2 dozen zwieback or rusks.*

|       |                                                      |
|-------|------------------------------------------------------|
| 1     | cup milk, scalded and cooled to slightly warmer than body temperature |
| 2     | Tbsp butter                                          |
| 1     | tsp malt syrup or molasses                           |
| 2     | eggs, slightly beaten                                |
| 1     | Tbsp or pkg dry yeast                                |
| 1     | Tbsp wheat germ                                      |
| ½     | tsp salt                                             |
| 1     | Tbsp soy flour                                       |
| 1     | Tbsp brown sugar                                     |
| ½     | tsp cinnamon (optional)                              |
| ½     | tsp nutmeg (optional)                                |
| 3–3½  | cups sifted unbleached white flour                   |

Scald 1 cup milk. Add 2 Tbsp butter and 1 tsp malt syrup or molasses and cool to a little warmer than body temperature. When mixture has cooled, add 2 slightly beaten eggs.

In medium-size bowl combine 1 Tbsp or pkg dry yeast, 1 Tbsp wheat germ, ½ tsp salt, 1 Tbsp soy flour, 1 Tbsp brown sugar with lumps broken up, ½ tsp cinnamon (optional), ½ tsp nutmeg (optional), and 2 cups white flour.

In bowl work liquid ingredients into dry ingredients by stirring and kneading, adding additional flour to make soft, slightly sticky dough. Let stand in warm place (75°–80°) to rise until double in bulk (about 2 hours).

Roll dough out in rectangle 3½–4 inches wide and as long as baking sheet. It should be about 1 inch thick. Put on baking sheet and bake in preheated 375° oven for about 1 hour or until light golden brown. Allow to cool on rack, cut crosswise into strips about ½ inch thick, and spread on baking sheet, cut sides up. Return to oven and bake at very low temperature, turning often, until rusks are bisque-colored and completely dried out (3–4 hours).

---

# Yeast-rising Flat Breads

# MIDDLE EASTERN POCKET BREAD

*Makes 12 loaves.* Excellent for sandwiches, especially those stuffed with egg salad or other sandwich salads. Also good served with Indian, Chinese, and, of course, Middle Eastern dishes.

| | |
|---:|:---|
| 1 | Tbsp or pkg dry yeast |
| 3 | Tbsp sugar |
| 2 | cups water, body temperature |
| 5½–6 | cups sifted unbleached white flour |
| ¼ | cup soy flour |
| 2 | tsp salt |
| ¼ | cup wheat germ |

In large bowl stir 1 Tbsp or pkg dry yeast and 1 Tbsp sugar into ½ cup water, body temperature. Set aside until sugar-yeast solution starts to foam (about 10 minutes).

Sift 5½ cups white flour, ¼ cup soy flour, 2 tsp salt, and 2 Tbsp sugar into medium-size bowl. Add ¼ cup wheat germ and mix thoroughly.

Add 1½ cups water, body temperature, to sugar-yeast solution in large bowl.

Gradually add dry ingredients to liquid. Stir with wooden spoon and then knead in bowl, adding additional flour if necessary. Dough should be only a little sticky. Or remove dough to lightly floured board and let rest while you wash, dry, and grease large bowl. Continue to knead until dough is elastic but still slightly sticky.

Form dough into ball and return to greased bowl, turning until well greased. Cover and set in warm place (70°–80°) free from drafts about 1 hour or until double in bulk.

Punch dough down and turn out onto bread board. Cut dough into 12 equal parts and form each into ball. Set aside, covered, for 10 minutes.

Preheat oven to 450°.

Pat or roll out balls of dough to about $1/4$–$1/3$ inch thick. Place on ungreased baking sheet and bake for 6–10 minutes or until light brown and puffy.

*Note:* If using gas oven, loaves can be placed directly on floor of oven. These will bake a little quicker.

Remove from oven, place on board, and cover loaves with towel. As bread cools, steam will escape and loaves will flatten, leaving pocket under top crust. Towel keeps loaves from drying out while steam escapes.

# PIZZA

*Makes 2 pizzas.* This recipe for dough, sauce, and topping is delicious, using a higher grade of ingredients than most commercial versions. We suggest sautéed mushrooms and peppers for topping, but you can choose your favorite garnish. The two cheeses, however, are a must.

*Dough*

| | |
|---|---|
| 1 | Tbsp or pkg dry yeast |
| 1 | cup water, body temperature |
| 2 | tsp sugar |
| 2 | Tbsp soy flour |
| 1 | Tbsp wheat germ |
| 1 | tsp salt |
| $2\frac{1}{4}$–$2\frac{1}{2}$ | cups sifted unbleached white flour |
| $1\frac{1}{2}$ | Tbsp melted butter |

In small bowl sprinkle 1 Tbsp or pkg dry yeast over 1 cup water, body temperature. Add 2 tsp sugar. Stir and set aside in warm place until bubbly (about 10 minutes).

In medium-size bowl combine 2 Tbsp soy flour, 1 Tbsp wheat germ, 1 tsp salt and 2 cups white flour. Melt 1½ Tbsp butter and add to combined flour mixture. Add bubbly yeast mixture and beat and blend until all flour is absorbed. Add additional flour as necessary to gain nonsticky soft dough. As dough begins to come away from sides of bowl, turn out onto floured bread board and knead until smooth.

Let dough rest while you wash, dry, and lightly grease bowl. Round dough up and place in bowl, turning dough so that it will be uniformly greased. Cover and set in warm place (70°–80°) free from drafts until double in bulk (about 1 hour).

*Make and prepare sauce and topping for pizza, directions for which are below, while dough is rising.*

Turn dough out onto floured board and punch down. Divide dough in half and shape each half into ball.

Preheat oven to 450°.

Roll out first ball and pull with fingers to make large circle about ⅛–¼ inch thick, or to your own taste.

Carefully put dough on lightly greased baking sheet. With large spoon or cup spread sauce evenly over dough, leaving ½-inch edge uncovered. Sprinkle Parmesan and mozzarella cheese over pizza first, then distribute mushrooms and peppers over the cheese. Put in middle of oven and bake 20–25 minutes

or until done to your satisfaction. (We don't recommend baking 2 pizzas at once if it means placing them on 2 racks, one over the other.) Cut into 8 pie-shaped pieces and serve hot.

Repeat for second pizza.

*Sauce*

|   |   |
|---|---|
| 2 | Tbsp olive oil |
| 1 | small onion, chopped |
| 1 | small garlic clove, minced or crushed |
| 1 | 14-ounce can Italian tomatoes, chopped but not drained, or 1⅔–2 cups fresh tomatoes, chopped |
| ½ | 6-ounce can tomato paste |
| 1 | tsp dried oregano or 2 tsp fresh oregano |
| 1 | tsp dried basil or 2 tsp fresh basil |
| 1 | tsp dried parsley or 2 tsp fresh parsley |
| 1 | bay leaf |
| ½ | tsp sugar |
| ½ | tsp salt |
| ¼ | tsp pepper |

Heat 2 Tbsp olive oil in large saucepan and sauté chopped onion and garlic. Add chopped tomatoes, ½ can tomato paste, oregano, basil, parsley, bay leaf, ½ tsp sugar, ½ tsp salt, and ¼ tsp pepper. Simmer sauce, stirring occasionally, until sauce thickens or about 45 minutes.

While sauce is cooking prepare ingredients for topping.

*Topping*

|   |   |
|---|---|
| ¼ | cup coarsely grated Parmesan cheese |
| ¼ | cup coarsely grated mozzarella cheese |
| ¼ | cup sliced and sautéed mushrooms (optional) |
| ½ | green pepper sliced and parboiled until softened (optional) |

# Yeast-rising
# Batter Breads

# HONEY-MOLASSES OATMEAL BREAD

*Makes 1 large loaf or 2 medium loaves.* Try to wait until cool to eat, but very good while still warm. We haven't found anyone who can resist this delicious, moist, fragrant bread. Fantastic as French Toast too.

|  |  |
|---|---|
| ¾ | cup rolled oats |
| 2 | tsp salt |
| 1½ | cups boiling water |
| 4 | Tbsp butter or oil |
| 2 | Tbsp molasses |
| 3 | Tbsp honey |
| ⅓ | cup water, body temperature |
| 1 | Tbsp or pkg dry yeast |
| 3 | cups sifted unbleached white flour |
| ¼ | cup wheat germ |
| ¼ | cup soy flour |
| ½ | cup whole wheat flour |
|  | Cornmeal |

In middle-size bowl put ¾ cup oatmeal (rolled oats or other), 2 tsp salt, and 1½ cups boiling water. Stir in 4 Tbsp butter or oil, 2 Tbsp molasses, 3 Tbsp honey. Cool to body temperature.

In ⅓ cup water, body temperature, sprinkle 1 Tbsp or pkg dry yeast. Stir to dissolve and set aside.

In large mixing bowl place 3 cups white flour and ¼ cup wheat germ. Sift in ¼ cup soy flour, ½ cup whole wheat flour and mix well.

When oatmeal mixture has cooled to body temperature, add yeast mixture and stir. Then add liquid mixture to dry ingredients all at once. Stir with wooden spoon until thick, elastic, rather sticky batter is formed.

Cover bowl with towel or plastic, and set in warm place (70°–80°) free from drafts until double in bulk (about 45 minutes).

Stir vigorously until gas is out of batter. Grease 1 large or

2 medium-size bread pans and sprinkle bottom and sides with cornmeal. Place batter in pan(s), filling half full, and smooth top with wet rubber spatula or wet fingers.

Cover with plastic or towel and set in warm place (70°–80°) free from drafts until batter rises almost to top of pan (about 45 minutes to 1 hour).

Preheat oven to 450° and turn down to 400° after putting in bread. Bake 50 minutes for medium-size loaves, longer for large, or until dark brown on top, and loaf sounds hollow when rapped with knuckle.

Remove from pan and cool on wire rack.

## WHOLE WHEAT BATTER BREAD

*Makes 2 medium loaves or 1 medium loaf and 4 mini loaves.* This is the bread that won the hearts of hundreds, reaping comments like—"Now you really have something" (a gourmet fifteen-year-old) ; and "He didn't complain when he came home from school!" (the mother of a seven-year-old boy who had taken it to school in his lunchbox). Diana's husband, Oscar, takes this bread along to work as mini loaves. It's good for lunch, dinner, or anytime—alone or with cheese.

|  |  |
|---|---|
| 3 | cups skim milk, or 1½ cups whole milk mixed with 1½ cups water, scalded and cooled to body temperature |
| 2 | Tbsp or pkgs dry yeast |
| ½ | cup water, body temperature |
| 6–6½ | cups whole wheat flour (about 2 pounds) |
| ½ | cup soy flour |
| ¼ | cup wheat germ |
| ¼ | cup brewer's yeast |
| 1½ | Tbsp salt |
| ¼ | cup brown sugar |
| ¼ | cup molasses |
| 2 | Tbsp corn oil |
|  | Cornmeal |

Scald 3 cups skim milk (or 1½ cups whole milk and 1½ cups water). Set aside to cool.

While milk is cooling stir 2 Tbsp or pkgs dry yeast into ½ cup water, body temperature. Set aside.

In large mixing bowl measure 6 cups (about 2 pounds) whole wheat flour. Add ½ cup soy flour, ¼ cup wheat germ, ¼ cup brewer's yeast, and 1½ Tbsp salt. Mix thoroughly.

When milk is cooled to body temperature, stir in yeast mixture, ¼ cup brown sugar, and ¼ cup molasses. Stir, then add 2 Tbsp corn oil.

Add liquid ingredients to dry mixture and stir for at least 5–10 minutes, if you have the strength and endurance. Batter should be very thick. Add up to ½ cup additional flour, if necessary.

Grease 2 medium-size bread pans or 1 medium and 4 mini pans, and sprinkle cornmeal on bottoms and sides.

Fill pans ½ full only, and set aside, covered, in warm place (75°–80°) for about 1 hour or longer, until batter rises to within 1 inch of top of pans (bread will not rise any more when placed in oven).

Gently lift pans and put into cold oven. Turn on oven (if gas oven, let fumes escape before closing door), set oven for 375°, and bake for 45 minutes to 1 hour, depending on size of pans used. *Do not look in oven before 30 minutes have passed, as this bread falls easily.* It is still good, though, even if fallen.

At end of 45 minutes, remove mini loaves, but continue baking larger loaves for additional 15–20 minutes. Loaves should sound hollow when rapped with knuckle.

Remove from pans and cool on racks.

*Rolls*

# BASIC DINNER ROLL DOUGH

*Makes 20–30 rolls.* This dough can be kept in the refrigerator for up to 3 days, warmed to room temperature, and formed into rolls. Diana's husband says it tastes like the rolls his mother used to make.

| | |
|---|---|
| 1 | cup milk, scalded and cooled to body temperature |
| 2 | Tbsp butter |
| 1 | egg, slightly beaten |
| 2 | Tbsp or pkgs dry yeast |
| ½ | cup water, body temperature |
| ¼ | cup light brown sugar |
| 2 | tsp salt |
| ¼ | cup soy flour |
| ¼ | cup wheat germ |
| About 5 | cups sifted unbleached white flour |

In saucepan scald 1 cup milk, add 2 Tbsp butter, and cool to body temperature. When sufficiently cooled, stir in 1 slightly beaten egg. Set aside.

In small container sprinkle 2 Tbsp or pkgs dry yeast over ½ cup water, body temperature. Stir. Set aside.

In large bowl combine ¼ cup light brown sugar with the lumps broken up, 2 tsp salt, ¼ cup soy flour, ¼ cup wheat germ, and 1 cup white flour.

Combine liquid ingredients and pour into dry ingredients. Beat until smooth. Stir in additional white flour until dough forms into ball. Turn out onto floured board and knead until smooth and elastic. Wash, dry, and grease bowl. Return dough to bowl, turning so that greased side is up. Cover with plastic and let rise in warm place (70°–80°) free from drafts until double in bulk, usually less than 1 hour. Or refrigerate dough for 2–3 days (longer and it will turn sour).

Punch down in bowl. (If dough has been refrigerated, warm to room temperature before punching down.) Form rolls—see directions that follow for different shapes. Cover and let rise in warm place (70°–80°) free from drafts until double in bulk, about 1 hour or less.

Bake all rolls in preheated 400° oven for 10 minutes; turn oven down to 350° and continue baking for 20 minutes, or until rolls are light brown. Serve hot.

## ROLL SHAPES

You can shape rolls from most of the kneaded yeast bread doughs we have described. It may, however, be necessary to add a little more flour to the dough. Or use Basic Dinner Roll Dough for your first efforts at shaping rolls. Choose the shapes that please you best or suit the occasion.

Sandwich Bun

Pull off pieces of dough 3 inches in diameter. Place on greased baking sheet about 2 inches apart and press to flatten.

Snails

Pull off pieces of dough about 3 inches in diameter. Form rope about ½ inch in diameter and 8–10 inches long. Holding 1 end down on greased baking sheet coil rope around and around and tuck end underneath. Brush with beaten egg or melted butter.

## Knots

Pull off pieces of dough about 3 inches in diameter. Form rope about 5 inches long. Holding rope at one end, make loop and pull the other end through to make knot. Now pull longer end through center of knot. Place on greased baking sheet and brush with melted butter.

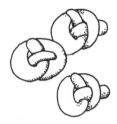

## Clover Leaf

Pull off pieces of dough a little less than 1 inch in diameter. Form into balls and place 3 or 4 in greased muffin cup. Brush with melted butter.

## Fan Tans

Roll dough into rectangle 1/4 inch thick. Brush with melted butter. Cut into long strips about 1¾ inches wide. Stack strips evenly and cut into squares. Place in greased muffin cups with cut side down.

## Crescents or Butterhorns

Roll ball of dough into a circle ¼ inch thick. Brush with melted butter. Cut into pie-shaped pieces or wedges. Starting at largest part, roll up toward point. Place on greased baking sheet, point underneath. For crescent shape, bend in curve.

# English Muffins

# ENGLISH MUFFINS AND ENGLISH
# MUFFIN BREAD

*Makes 10 English Muffins.* Double recipe to make 10 English Muffins and 1 loaf English Muffin Bread or to make 2 loaves English Muffin Bread. These muffins are delicious and slices of English Muffin Bread make excellent toast. (For directions on how to make your own English Muffin cutter, see page 202.)

1 Tbsp or pkg dry yeast
1 cup water, body temperature
1 Tbsp sugar
1 tsp salt
2 Tbsp farina
2 Tbsp nonfat dry milk
3 cups sifted unbleached white flour
1 Tbsp melted butter or oil
Cornmeal

In large bowl combine 1 Tbsp or pkg dry yeast and 1 cup water, body temperature. Stir until dissolved and set aside.

Mix thoroughly 1 Tbsp sugar, 1 tsp salt, 2 Tbsp farina, 2 Tbsp nonfat dry milk, and 2½ cups white flour. Add dry mixture to liquid mixture. Add 1 Tbsp melted butter or oil and blend thoroughly.

When dough lifts away from sides of bowl, turn out onto lightly floured bread board or tabletop. Knead until smooth, adding flour as required. Place dough in lightly oiled bowl, turning oiled side up, cover, and let rise in warm place (70°–80°) free from drafts until double in bulk or about 1 hour. Punch down. (If you are doubling the recipe to make an English Muffin loaf in addition to muffins, divide dough at this point and see instructions below.)

Roll dough for muffins ¾ inch thick. With 3-inch circular cutter, cut out rounds. (A glass 3 inches in diameter or opened tin can with air holes in top may also be used.) Place rounds 1 inch apart on flat plates or baking sheet sprinkled with cornmeal. Turn over so that both sides are liberally coated with cornmeal. Cover and let rise until double in bulk, about 30 minutes.

Bake slowly on greased preheated griddle for about 15 minutes, turning once.

*Note:* Make dough the night before. After first rising, cut out muffins, cover loosely with cloth, refrigerate, and let rise slowly until next morning. Follow baking instructions and enjoy the best English Muffins you have ever tasted.

*English Muffin Bread:* From second half of dough, form loaf and place seam side down in large bread pan which has been greased and liberally sprinkled with cornmeal. Cover and let rise in warm place (70°–80°) until double in bulk or until dough reaches top of pan. Place in preheated 325° oven and bake for approximately 1 hour. Remove from pan and cool on rack.

*Yeast Breads*

# WHOLE WHEAT ENGLISH CREAM
# CHEESE MUFFINS

*Makes 8–10 English Muffins.* Ideal toasted for breakfast or lunch. If they turn out thick, cut them in 3 slices rather than 2. If you prefer, try this recipe using all unbleached white flour instead of whole wheat and white. (For directions on how to make your own English Muffin cutter, see page 202.)

| | |
|---|---|
| 1 | cup milk, scalded and cooled to body temperature |
| 1 | Tbsp or pkg dry yeast |
| 1 | tsp sugar |
| ¼ | cup water, body temperature |
| 4 | ounces softened cream cheese |
| 1 | egg |
| 1 | Tbsp salt |
| ¼ | cup brown sugar |
| 1 | cup whole wheat flour |
| 4–5 | cups sifted unbleached white flour |
| | Cornmeal |

Scald 1 cup milk and set aside to cool to body temperature.

In small bowl put 1 Tbsp or pkg dry yeast and 1 tsp sugar in ¼ cup water, body temperature, and stir. Set aside until mixture starts to bubble.

Using separate container, blend 4 ounces softened cream cheese, 1 egg, and 1 Tbsp salt. Set aside.

In large bowl mix together scalded milk, cooled to body temperature, ¼ cup brown sugar, and yeast mixture. Add 1 cup whole wheat flour and about 4 cups white flour. (More or less flour may be necessary depending upon absorbency of dough.) When dough starts to come away from sides of bowl, turn out onto floured board, working in as much additional flour as dough will take to make soft but not sticky dough.

---

Let dough rest a few minutes while you wash and dry bowl. *Do not grease bowl.* Form dough into ball, coat with flour and return to bowl. Cover and set in warm place (75°–80°) to rise until double in bulk (about 2–3 hours).

Gently turn dough out onto lightly floured board. Roll dough out to about 1/3–1/2 inch thick and sprinkle top generously with white or yellow cornmeal. Cut out muffins by pushing straight down with a 3-inch cutter. Place on baking sheet or large plate sprinkled with cornmeal. Cover with tent-like sheet of plastic (see page 48.) Let rise in warm place (75°–80°) until double in bulk, about 2–3 hours, or let rise overnight in refrigerator.

Bake slowly on preheated griddle about 7–10 minutes per side. Watch carefully so they do not become too brown. Serve immediately, or cool and store in freezer, and toast and serve at your convenience.

# *Bagels*

Joan was brought up on bagels—Sunday mornings with the comic strips, bagels, lox, cream cheese, and pickled herring—and so was particularly enthused about their addition to this book. But even Oscar, Diana's Texas-bred cornbread-fed husband, changed his negative opinion about the delicacy after trying these recipes.

# POTATO EGG BAGELS

*Makes about 15 or 16 bagels.* They'll compete with New York's finest.

|         |                                          |
|--------:|------------------------------------------|
| 1       | Tbsp or pkg dry yeast                    |
| 1       | cup potato water, body temperature (see page 25) |
| 3       | eggs, well beaten                        |
| 2       | tsp salt                                 |
| 2       | tsp brown sugar                          |
| 2       | Tbsp melted butter or oil                |
| ¼       | cup wheat germ                           |
| ¼       | cup soy flour                            |
| 4½–4¾   | cups sifted unbleached white flour       |
| 2       | Tbsp sugar                               |
| 2       | quarts boiling water                     |
|         | *Glaze:* 1 egg yolk beaten with 1 Tbsp water |

In small bowl sprinkle 1 Tbsp or pkg dry yeast over 1 cup potato water, body temperature. Stir and set aside.

In large mixing bowl vigorously beat 3 eggs. Add 2 tsp salt, 2 tsp brown sugar, and 2 Tbsp melted butter or oil. Blend in. Add yeast and potato water. Stir in ¼ cup wheat germ, ¼ cup soy flour, and 3 cups sifted white flour. Gradually add remaining flour until soft dough is formed which begins to separate from sides of bowl.

Turn out onto floured board. Let dough rest while you wash, dry, and grease bowl. Knead until dough is smooth, elastic, and firm, adding more flour as necessary to gain this consistency.

Form into ball and return dough to greased bowl, turning until well greased. Cover and put in warm place (70°–80°) to rise until double in bulk (about 1–1½ hours).

Punch dough down, knead a few times, and form into rectangle. Cut dough into 15 or 16 equal pieces. Roll each piece between palms of your hands to form rope about 5 inches long and ¾ inch thick. Seal ends together firmly (use a little water if necessary) and shape like doughnut. Place on board to rise about 20 minutes.

Dissolve 2 Tbsp sugar in 2 quarts boiling water. With spatula gently drop in bagels one at a time without crowding. (Boil 3 or 4 at a time, depending upon amount of room.) Bagels will almost immediately rise to surface. Turn over and boil 2–3 minutes longer. During this time bagels will expand and rise.

Carefully remove with spatula or slotted spoon and place bagels on greased baking sheet. Brush with egg yolk glaze. Bake in preheated 425° oven for about 25 minutes or until bagels are nice and brown.

Eat fresh out of the oven with butter, cream cheese and lox, or plain. To reheat, sprinkle bagels with a little water and place in preheated 400° oven for about 10 minutes. If frozen, leave them in oven about 20 minutes.


## WHOLE WHEAT BAGELS

*Makes 12–14 fair-size bagels.* These have a good whole wheat flavor.

|      |                                          |
| ---- | ---------------------------------------- |
| 1    | Tbsp or pkg dry yeast                    |
| 1    | cup potato water, body temperature       |
|      | (see page 25)                            |
| 3    | eggs, well beaten                        |
| 1    | Tbsp salt                                |
| 1    | Tbsp honey or molasses                   |
| 2    | Tbsp melted butter                       |
| ¼    | cup wheat germ                           |
| ¼    | cup soy flour                            |
| 2    | cups whole wheat flour                   |

2   cups sifted unbleached white flour
2   Tbsp sugar
2   quarts boiling water
    *Glaze:* 1 egg yolk beaten with 1 Tbsp water

In small bowl sprinkle 1 Tbsp or pkg dry yeast over 1 cup potato water, body temperature. Stir and set aside.

In large bowl vigorously beat 3 eggs. Add 1 Tbsp salt, 1 Tbsp honey or molasses, and 2 Tbsp melted butter. Add yeast and potato water. Stir.

In medium-size bowl combine 1/4 cup wheat germ, sift in 1/4 cup soy flour, 2 cups whole wheat flour, and 2 cups white flour.

Gradually add dry ingredients to liquid until soft dough is formed which begins to separate from sides of bowl.

Turn out onto floured board. Let dough rest while you wash, dry, and grease bowl. Knead dough until smooth, elastic, and moderately firm, adding more flour as necessary.

Form into ball and return dough to greased bowl, turning until greased. Cover and put in warm place (75°–80°) free from drafts to rise until double in bulk (4–6 hours). It is possible to leave dough out overnight to rise at a slightly lower temperature.

Punch dough down, knead a few times, and divide dough into 12–14 equal parts. Roll each piece between palms of your hands to form rope about 5 inches long and 3/4 inch thick. Seal ends together firmly, using a little water, and shape like doughnut. Place on board and let rise about 20 minutes.

Dissolve 2 Tbsp sugar in 2 quarts boiling water. Using spatula, gently drop in bagels one at a time but do not crowd pot. Bagels will almost immediately rise to surface. Turn over and boil 2–3 minutes longer. During this time bagels will expand and rise.

Remove and place on greased baking sheet. Brush with egg yolk glaze. Bake in preheated 425° oven for about 20–25 minutes or until browned to your satisfaction.

Serve immediately, or cool and toast, or reheat in oven.

---

*Yeast Breads*                                      153

# RYE POTATO FLOUR BAGELS

*Makes about 15 or 16 bagels.* Our rye bagels rise very nicely, too.

|        |                                         |
|--------|-----------------------------------------|
| 1      | Tbsp or pkg dry yeast                   |
| 1      | cup water, body temperature             |
| 3      | eggs, well beaten                       |
| 2      | Tbsp melted butter or oil               |
| ¼      | cup potato flour                        |
| ¼      | cup soy flour                           |
| 1½     | cups rye flour                          |
| 3–3½   | cups sifted unbleached white flour      |
| 1½     | Tbsp salt                               |
| 1      | Tbsp brown sugar or honey               |
| 1      | Tbsp dried orange peel                  |
| 1      | Tbsp caraway seeds                      |
| 2      | Tbsp sugar                              |
| 2      | quarts boiling water                    |
|        | *Glaze:* 1 egg yolk beaten with 1 Tbsp water |

In small bowl sprinkle 1 Tbsp or pkg dry yeast over 1 cup water, body temperature. Stir and set aside.

In large mixing bowl beat 3 eggs vigorously and blend in 2 Tbsp melted butter or oil.

In medium-size bowl combine ¼ cup potato flour, ¼ cup soy flour, 1½ cups rye flour, and about 2 cups white flour. Add 1½ Tbsp salt, 1 Tbsp brown sugar with lumps broken up or honey, 1 Tbsp dried orange peel, and 1 Tbsp caraway seeds.

Add yeast solution to eggs in large bowl. Gradually add in combined flours until soft dough is formed. When dough starts to separate from sides of bowl, turn out onto lightly floured board. Let dough rest while you wash, dry, and grease mixing bowl.

Knead dough, adding additional flour as needed to make firm dough. Return to greased bowl, turning to grease all over, cover, and set in warm place (75°–80°) free from drafts to rise until double in bulk (about 2–3 hours).

Punch dough down, turn out onto board, and knead a few times. Form into rectangle and cut dough into 15 or 16 equal pieces. Roll each piece between palms of your hands to form rope about 5 inches long and ¾ inch thick. Seal ends together firmly (a little water may be necessary) to form doughnut shape. Place on board to rise about 20 minutes.

Dissolve 2 Tbsp sugar in 2 quarts boiling water. With spatula gently drop bagels into boiling water one at a time without crowding. When bagels rise to surface, turn over and continue boiling 2–3 minutes on second side. Bagels will rise and expand during this period in boiling water.

Carefully remove bagels with spatula or slotted spoon and place on greased baking sheet. Brush with egg yolk glaze. Bake in preheated 425° oven for about 25 minutes or until golden brown.

# *Doughnuts*

## GENERAL HINTS

When shaping doughnuts using any of the recipes that follow, divide your mixture into thirds and deal with one third at a time for easier handling, incorporating scraps in the next batch. Knead slightly. Then pat or roll dough out to 1/3–1/2 inch thick. Cut with a floured, sharp doughnut cutter. Knead, roll, and shape remaining mixture in the same way.

## CRULLERS OR TWISTS

Add additional flour to yeast doughnut recipe to make dough stiff and then pat dough out into a rectangle 10 inches long and 1/2 inch thick. Cut strips about 3/4 inch wide and shape into twists or figure 8's, pinching ends tightly together. Drop into hot fat or place on baking sheet to be put in the oven when light.

## FRYING DOUGHNUTS

When you fry doughnuts it is important to keep oil temperature at 375°. You can test the temperature with a deep-frying thermometer or by dropping a small piece of dough into the oil. If it turns golden brown in 60 seconds, the oil is about right. Fry doughnuts 3 or 4 at a time—no more. If you crowd the pan, the oil temperature drops and doughnuts will absorb too much fat—they'll be greasy. If temperature is too hot, doughnuts brown before they rise or cook inside. When dough-nuts rise to the surface, turn them over to brown on the other side. When brown on both sides, remove from pan with slotted spoon, skewer, or fork and drain on paper towels or brown paper.

*Recycling Oil.* While your oil is still hot, slip a few slices of raw potato into the pot (about 4 slices to 1 quart oil) and heat until it bubbles. (Potato absorbs flavor and collects some of the sediment.) Discard potato slices and let oil cool—remaining sediment will settle on the bottom. Strain oil carefully through a wire strainer lined with 2 or 3 layers of cheesecloth. Pour into lightproof container, cover tightly, and refrigerate.


## SUGARING AND GLAZING

Doughnuts and crullers or twists are good plain, sugared, or glazed.


### Sugar Doughnuts

Shake one at a time in paper bag with a little confectioners' sugar, granulated sugar, or sugar and cinnamon mixed.


### Boiled Chocolate Glaze

Put 2 squares or ounces unsweetened chocolate into saucepan and melt without scorching. Stir in 3 Tbsp milk or cream and 1 Tbsp water. Mix well and add about ½ cup confectioners' sugar. Boil about 5 minutes. While mixture is hot, spread evenly over surface of cooled doughnuts.

*If boiled frosting is not stiff enough when ready to spread,* set bowl or saucepan containing mixture over lower part of double boiler or pot containing boiling water and place over heat. Stir until mixture just begins to become granular around edges. Remove from heat immediately and beat mixture with a spoon until it will hold its shape. Pour or spread on doughnuts, etc.

Almond Glaze

Beat 1 egg white until stiff. Pulverize 1 cup almonds in blender with 1 cup confectioners' sugar into fine paste. Add egg white and a few drops of vanilla extract. Blend a few minutes to mix thoroughly and spread on doughnuts or crullers.

Plain Glaze

Beat 1 egg white until stiff. Add 2 tsp cold water and about ¾ cup confectioners' sugar. Beat thoroughly, adding ½ tsp vanilla extract or ½ Tbsp lemon juice. Use additional sugar to gain right consistency, which should be fairly thick.

# BAKED DOUGHNUTS

*Makes about 24 doughnuts.* Very good with or without glaze, made especially for those who don't like fried foods.

|     |     |
| --- | --- |
| 1   | Tbsp or pkg dry yeast |
| 1   | cup water, body temperature |
| 1/2 | tsp sugar |
| 2 1/2 | cups sifted unbleached white flour |
| 1/4 | cup soy flour |
| 2   | Tbsp wheat germ |
| 1/4 | cup nonfat dry milk |
| 3   | Tbsp brown sugar |
| 1   | tsp salt |
| 1   | tsp nutmeg |
| 1   | tsp dried orange or lemon peel |
| 1   | egg or 2 egg yolks, slightly beaten |
| 4   | Tbsp melted butter |

In small bowl or measuring cup sprinkle 1 Tbsp or pkg dry yeast over 1/4 cup water, body temperature. Stir in 1/2 tsp sugar. Set aside until bubbling.

Combine in large mixing bowl 2 1/2 cups white flour, 1/4 cup soy flour, 2 Tbsp wheat germ, 1/4 cup nonfat dry milk, 3 Tbsp brown sugar with lumps broken up, 1 tsp salt, 1 tsp nutmeg, and 1 tsp dried orange or lemon peel. Mix dry ingredients well.

Add bubbling yeast mixture to dry ingredients along with 1 egg or 2 egg yolks, slightly beaten, 3 Tbsp melted butter, and 3/4 cup water, body temperature.

Beat and knead mixture in bowl. Dough should be only stiff enough to handle. If it is too moist add a *little* additional flour.

Cover bowl and let rise in warm place (70°–80°) free from drafts until double in bulk, about 45 minutes to 1 hour.

Turn out onto board and knead a few times. Pat dough out about 1/2 inch thick. With floured doughnut cutter cut out rings and place carefully on greased baking sheet. You can bake centers also.

---

Cover and let rise in warm place (70°–80°) until very light, about 30 minutes. Brush lightly (feather brush is excellent to use) with remaining 1 Tbsp melted butter before baking in preheated 400° oven for about 15–20 minutes or until well browned.

Remove from oven. Glaze or sugar them while hot.

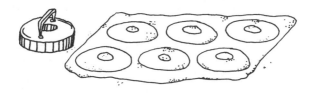

## GERMAN DOUGHNUTS

*Makes 20–30 doughnuts.* These unusual doughnuts are tough and chewy on the outside while soft on the inside. We enjoy them best with confectioners' sugar or a mixture of sugar and cinnamon.

|  |  |
|---|---|
| 1 | cup scalded milk |
| 2 | tsp butter |
| About 3½ | cups sifted unbleached white flour |
| 1 | tsp nutmeg, cloves or allspice |
| ½ | tsp salt |
| 2 | eggs, separated |
|  | Peanut oil for deep-frying |

Scald 1 cup milk and add 2 tsp butter. When butter has melted, pour mixture over 2½ cups white flour in medium-size bowl. Beat with wire whisk until smooth and let cool to body temperature.

Add 1 tsp nutmeg, cloves, or allspice, and ½ tsp salt. Separate 2 eggs and beat egg yolks until relatively light. Add to

---

dough, beating all the while. Beat egg whites until stiff and fold in.

Add enough additional flour to make soft dough. Turn out onto floured board and knead several times. Gently roll or pat dough out to ½-inch thickness. Cut strips 4 inches long and about ½ inch wide. Twist each strip and pinch ends together to make circle.

In large pot heat 4–5 inches peanut oil to 375°. Lower 3 or 4 doughnuts at a time gently into oil. Turn them frequently so they will rise and brown evenly (about 5–6 minutes for doughnuts, 10 minutes for crullers). Remove doughnuts from oil with slotted spoon, skewer, or fork, and drain on brown paper or paper towels.

## WHOLE WHEAT DOUGHNUTS

*Makes about 2½ dozen doughnuts.* We prefer them with confectioners' sugar, but they're good with chocolate or almond glaze as well.

|       |                                    |
| ----- | ---------------------------------- |
| 1     | cup water, body temperature        |
| ½     | tsp sugar                          |
| 1     | Tbsp or pkg dry yeast              |
| 4–5   | cups sifted unbleached white flour |
| 3     | eggs, well beaten                  |
| ¼     | cup dark brown sugar or molasses   |
| ½     | tsp vanilla                        |
| ¼     | cup melted butter                  |
| ¼     | tsp allspice                       |
| 2     | tsp dried orange or lime peel      |
| 1     | tsp salt                           |
| 1     | cup whole wheat flour              |
|       | Peanut oil for deep-frying         |

In large mixing bowl mix 1 cup water, body temperature, with ½ tsp sugar and 1 Tbsp or pkg dry yeast. Stir and set aside. Beat in with wire whisk 1 cup white flour and let this sponge stand 1 hour in warm place (80°) to rise.

In medium-size container vigorously beat 3 eggs. Add ¼ cup dark brown sugar with lumps broken up, or molasses, ½ tsp vanilla, ¼ cup melted butter, ¼ tsp allspice, 2 tsp dried orange or lime peel, and 1 tsp salt. Mix with wire whisk or beater until well blended.

Pour egg mixture into sponge along with 1 cup whole wheat flour. Stir, adding white flour in ½-cup amounts until dough starts to come away from sides of bowl. Spread ½–1 cup of flour on board, turn dough out, and knead, using more flour as needed to make smooth and satiny dough. Let dough rest while you wash, dry, and grease bowl. Round dough up into ball. Put in bowl, turning greased side up, cover with towel, and let rise in warm place (80°) until double in bulk (about 1½ hours). If you have time, punch dough down, round up, and let rise again.

Turn dough out onto board, knead about 6 times, and roll out dough about ½ inch thick. Cut with doughnut cutter, or cut strips for twists or crullers, and place on lightly floured board. Cover with a thin cloth and let rise in a warm place (80°) about 1 hour, or until double in bulk.

In large pot heat about 4½–5 inches peanut oil to 375°. Carefully slip doughnuts into hot fat 3 or 4 at a time. Don't crowd! As they rise to surface and brown, turn over and brown on other side. When brown on both sides, lift out with spatula, slotted spoon, skewer, or fork and drain on paper towels or brown paper. Roll in sugar while still warm, or glaze.

Eat warm or freeze, tightly wrapped. These doughnuts never become hard.

---

# BAKING POWDER DOUGHNUTS

*Makes about 2½ dozen doughnuts.* Baking powder doughnuts are somewhat quicker to make than yeast-rising doughnuts but the final product, while light, does not rise as much as dough-nuts made with yeast.

|     |                                         |
| --- | --------------------------------------- |
| 3   | eggs                                    |
| 1   | cup light or dark brown sugar           |
| 2   | Tbsp soft butter                        |
| ¼   | cup wheat germ                          |
| ¼   | cup soy flour                           |
| 1   | tsp mace, nutmeg, or cinnamon           |
| 1   | tsp salt                                |
| 3   | tsp baking powder                       |
| 3¼  | cups sifted unbleached white flour      |
| ⅔   | cup milk or buttermilk                  |
|     | Peanut oil for deep-frying              |

In large bowl cream 3 eggs, 1 cup brown sugar with lumps broken up, and 2 Tbsp butter until light and fluffy. Set aside.

In medium-size bowl combine ¼ cup wheat germ, ¼ cup soy flour, 1 tsp mace, nutmeg, or cinnamon, 1 tsp salt, 3 tsp baking powder, and 3¼ cups white flour.

Beat ⅔ cup milk or buttermilk into egg-sugar mixture. Gradually add flour mixture, stirring, beating, and then knead-ing until soft dough forms. Cover with plastic or damp towel and refrigerate until cold (1–2 hours), as dough is easier to work.

Divide dough in half, returning one half to refrigerator until ready to be rolled. Turn dough out onto well-floured board and roll out ⅓ inch thick. Cut with doughnut cutter, dipping cutter into flour before each cutting. Carefully place doughnuts on lightly floured plate, second board, or pastry cloth as you cut them out.

Heat oil in pot (using 4–5 inches of oil). When temperature

reaches 375° or piece of dough dropped in rises to surface immediately and begins to brown, carefully drop in doughnuts 3 or 4 at a time. (Too many will cool oil too much.)

As they rise to surface and brown, turn them over so that they will brown on other side; fry about 3–4 minutes in all. Remove from oil and drain on paper towels or brown paper. Glaze or shake in confectioners' sugar or cinnamon-sugar mixture.

*Note:* If you wish to make whole wheat baking powder doughnuts, substitute 1 cup whole wheat flour for an equal amount of white flour; increase amount of milk from ⅔ cup to ¾ cup; and increase amount of baking powder from 3 tsp to 4 tsp. They will be nice too.

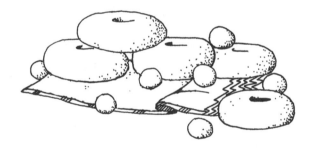

# Quick Breads

# NEEDED AND UNKNEADED

Quick breads are made with quick-acting leavening such as baking powder and/or baking soda and an acid, or steam, rather than yeast, so the rising time is eliminated. Many of them are batter breads that require no kneading—a fact that makes them popular with bread makers who don't want to get their hands messy.

The breads that are baked in the oven include tea breads, popovers, muffins, biscuits, scones. Pancakes and waffles—also quick breads—are baked on a griddle or in a skillet.

We enjoy these breads anytime and they are quick and easy to make.

*In our recipes, a large loaf pan is 9 × 5 × 3 inches, a medium loaf pan is 8½ × 4½ × 2½ inches, a small loaf pan is 8 × 4 × 2¼ inches, and a mini pan is 5½ × 3 × 2 inches.*

# Tea Breads

Tea breads should be eaten soon after baking—they are at their best the first day. You will be using fruits, nuts, vegetables and spices, and will experience a variety of bread textures.

# RYE BANANA NUT BREAD

*Makes 1 large loaf or 4 mini loaves.* Delicious plain, or with butter or cream cheese, or slightly toasted—particularly at teatime or for a midnight snack.

| | |
|---|---|
| 3 | medium or 2 large ripe bananas |
| 2 | Tbsp lemon juice |
| ½ | cup butter |
| 1 | cup white sugar or 1 cup light brown sugar |
| 2 | eggs, slightly beaten |
| 1¾ | cups sifted unbleached white flour |
| ½ | cup rye flour |
| 2 | Tbsp wheat germ |
| 2 | Tbsp soy flour |
| 1½ | tsp baking powder |
| ½ | tsp baking soda |
| ½ | tsp salt |
| ¾ | cup walnuts, pecans, or your favorite kind of nuts |
| 1 | tsp chopped candied ginger (optional) |

Preheat oven to 375°.

Liquefy in blender or mash thoroughly in bowl 2 large or 3 medium-size bananas, adding 2 Tbsp lemon juice to prevent mixture from turning brown.

In large bowl, using electric hand mixer or wooden spoon, cream ½ cup butter and 1 cup sugar until smooth. Add 2 beaten eggs, continuing to blend. Now add bananas to butter, sugar, and eggs and blend until smooth.

In another bowl mix together 1¾ cup white flour, ½ cup rye flour, 2 Tbsp wheat germ, 2 Tbsp soy flour, 1½ tsp baking powder, ½ tsp baking soda, and ½ tsp salt. Stir with fork until mixture is well blended.

Gradually add dry mixture to liquid mixture, blending as long as possible with electric hand mixer and then wooden spoon (or using wooden spoon entirely).

When well mixed, dough will be a little stiff but still liquid.

---

Add nuts and, for slightly exotic taste (which should be tried), 1 tsp finely chopped candied ginger.

Grease 1 large loaf pan or 4 mini loaf pans with butter or margarine. Spoon batter into pan(s) and bake in preheated oven until toothpick or cake tester comes out clean when thrust into center of bread. If using mini loaf pans bake at 350° for about 1 hour. If using large loaf pan bake at 375° for about 1¼ hours. *Cool in pans*, then remove carefully.

## BLUEBERRY TEA LOAF

*Makes 2 medium loaves or 1 medium loaf and 4 mini loaves.* A treat any time of day and with almost any meal. Also good served with a little confectioners' sugar.

| | |
|---|---|
| 2½ | cups whole wheat flour |
| 2½ | cups sifted unbleached white flour |
| 4 | tsp baking powder |
| ½ | tsp salt |
| 1 | cup butter, softened |
| 2 | cups dark brown sugar |
| 4 | eggs |
| 2 | cups milk |
| 2 | cups fresh blueberries, |
| | or thawed frozen blueberries, drained |

Preheat oven to 350°.

In medium-size bowl combine 2½ cups whole wheat flour, 2½ cups white flour, 4 tsp baking powder, and ½ tsp salt.

In large bowl cream together with electric beater or rotary beater 1 cup butter and 2 cups dark brown sugar with lumps broken up. Add 4 eggs and beat until smooth and light.

Gradually add and blend in flour mixture and milk alternately, beating until smooth.

*Start* With wooden spoon or spatula gently fold in 2 cups blueberries. Pour batter into greased medium-size bread pans or mini pans. Place in preheated 350° oven and bake medium-size loaves about 1¼–1½ hours or until done when tested with cake tester. Mini loaves take about 65 minutes to bake.

*Cool in pans* for about 30 minutes. Gently remove and serve slightly warm with a little confectioners' sugar sprinkled on top, or cool completely.


## SWEET POTATO BREAD

*Makes 1 large loaf or 4 mini loaves.* This tea bread tastes a lot like gingerbread but has a more cake-like texture. For a change, try canned or cooked pumpkin in season, in place of sweet potato.

|     |                                                           |
| --- | --------------------------------------------------------- |
| 2   | eggs, well beaten                                         |
| 1   | cup cooked or canned sweet potato,                        |
|     | mashed until soft or liquefied in blender                 |
| ½   | cup oil                                                   |
| ⅓   | cup cold water                                            |
| ½   | cup honey                                                 |
| 2   | cups sifted unbleached white flour                        |
| 2   | Tbsp soy flour                                            |
| 2   | Tbsp wheat germ                                           |
| 1   | Tbsp baking soda                                          |

1    Tbsp salt
½    tsp cinnamon
½    tsp nutmeg
1    cup brown sugar or white sugar

Preheat oven to 325°.

In medium-size bowl, using wire whisk, rotary beater, or wooden spoon, blend together 2 well-beaten eggs, 1 cup mashed sweet potato, ½ cup oil, ⅓ cup cold water, and ½ cup honey.

In large mixing bowl combine 2 cups white flour, 2 Tbsp soy flour, 2 Tbsp wheat germ, 1 Tbsp baking soda, 1 Tbsp salt, ½ tsp cinnamon, ½ tsp nutmeg, and 1 cup brown sugar with lumps broken up or white sugar.

Pour liquid ingredients into dry ingredients all at once and beat with wooden spoon until smooth.

Pour batter into 1 greased large bread pan or 4 greased mini pans and bake about 1½ hours for large loaf and 1 hour for mini loaves or until done when tested with cake tester, toothpick, or broomstraw.

Watch these loaves carefully, as they burn easily. They will come out a gingerbread color. *Cool in pan,* then remove carefully.

# NUTTIER DATE NUT BREAD

*Makes 2 medium loaves or 1 small loaf and 4 mini loaves.*
Nutty and moist with a nice fruity flavor. Excellent for serving with coffee or tea.

| | |
|---:|:---|
| 1½ | cups hot water |
| 1¼–1½ | cups pitted dates, cut up |
| ½ | cup molasses or ⅓ cup honey |
| ¼ | cup butter |
| 1 | cup dark brown sugar |
| 3 | eggs |
| ¼ | cup wheat germ |
| ¼ | cup soy flour |
| 2½ | tsp baking soda |
| 2 | tsp salt |
| ¼ | tsp nutmeg, or ground cloves, or allspice (optional) |
| 2 | cups whole wheat flour |
| 1½ | cups sifted unbleached white flour |
| 2 | cups walnuts, broken into large pieces |

Preheat oven to 325°.

In 4-cup measure or medium-size bowl pour 1½ cups hot water over 1¼–1½ cups pitted dates, cut up. Add ½ cup molasses or ⅓ cup honey and stir. Set aside.

In large bowl cream ¼ cup butter with 1 cup dark brown sugar with lumps broken up. Beat in 3 eggs. Pour in dates-molasses-hot water. Stir until well blended.

In medium-size bowl combine ¼ cup wheat germ, ¼ cup soy flour, 2½ tsp baking soda, 2 tsp salt, spices, if you like, 2 cups whole wheat flour, and 1½ cups white flour. Stir in 2 cups walnuts, coating them well with flour.

Gradually add dry ingredients to liquid 1 cup at a time, blending and stirring until thick batter forms. Spoon batter into 2 greased medium-size bread pans or 1 small and 4 mini pans.

Bake in preheated 325° oven 1 hour for mini loaves and 1¼ hours for medium-size loaves or until cake tester comes out clean when inserted into bread. *Cool in pans*, then remove carefully. Serve either cold or warm. Keeps very well in freezer too.

## COUNTRY GINGERBREAD

*Makes 9 servings or 4 mini loaves.* Gingerbread used to be unleavened, baked in shapes to look like crowns, cocks, kings, queens, and houses, and sold at county fairs. The hard gingerbread had a rather esoteric use as a weather indicator—the slightest moisture made it soft, but dry air made it tough and hard. The following recipe makes a soft gingerbread, lightened by baking soda. A note at the end tells you how to make your own edible "barometer."

|     |     |
| --- | --- |
| ½   | cup buttermilk |
| ½   | cup butter |
| ½   | cup dark brown sugar |
| ½   | cup molasses |
| 2   | eggs, separated |
| 1½  | cups sifted unbleached white flour |
| 1   | tsp baking soda |
| 1   | tsp cinnamon |
| 2   | tsp ginger |
| ¼   | tsp nutmeg (optional) |
| ¼   | tsp ground cloves (optional) |

In saucepan scald ½ cup buttermilk. Add ½ cup butter and set aside to cool to body temperature.
Preheat oven to 350°.

In large bowl combine ½ cup dark brown sugar with lumps broken up, ½ cup molasses, and yolks of 2 eggs. Beat until smooth and add cooled buttermilk-butter mixture.

Blend together in separate bowl 1½ cups white flour, 1 tsp baking soda, 1 tsp cinnamon, and 2 tsp ginger. You may add ¼ tsp nutmeg and ¼ tsp ground cloves, if you like, for more subtle flavoring.

Gradually add dry ingredients to liquid, beating all the while until smooth. Whip 2 egg whites in small bowl until stiff and fold into batter.

Pour batter into 1 greased 8-inch square pan or 4 greased mini pans. Bake in preheated 350° oven for about 1¼ hours or until done when tested with cake tester.

*Note:* For hard gingerbread biscuits or "people," use above recipe but omit eggs and mix in enough additional flour to make dough stiff enough to roll out like biscuits. Roll out ½ inch thick and cut out with biscuit cutter or "people" cutter. Bake on baking sheet. Remove from oven and, while hot, rub on a thin layer of molasses. Let cool.

## HONEY-GINGER BREAD

*Makes 1 small loaf.* Recipe can be doubled to make enough for 2 small loaf pans or 4 mini loaf pans. Bread is very moist, but great when toasted. Good when eaten cold too.

| | |
|---|---|
| 2 | cups sifted unbleached white flour |
| 1 | tsp baking soda |
| 1 | tsp baking powder |
| 1 | tsp salt |
| ½ | tsp cinnamon |
| 1 | tsp ginger |
| 1 | egg, slightly beaten |
| ½ | cup honey |
| 1 | cup milk, room temperature |

Preheat oven to 350°.

In large mixing bowl combine 2 cups white flour, 1 tsp baking soda, 1 tsp baking powder, 1 tsp salt, ½ tsp cinnamon, and 1 tsp ginger.

In medium-size bowl blend 1 slightly beaten egg with ½ cup honey and gradually beat in 1 cup milk, room temperature. You will find honey breaks down and finally blends evenly into mixture.

Pour liquid ingredients into large bowl with dry ingredients and beat thoroughly for about 15–20 minutes, thus giving batter a light and fine consistency. Pour batter into 1 greased small loaf pan.

Bake in preheated 350° oven for approximately 35–40 minutes or until top springs back when touched.

## ✓ LEMON BREAD

*Makes 1 large or 1 small loaf and 2 mini loaves.* The gentle aroma and taste of lemon plus crisp texture from walnut meats make this bread a delight.

| | |
|---|---|
| 1¼ | cups whole wheat flour |
| 1¼ | cups unsifted unbleached white flour |
| ¼ | cup soy flour |
| 2 | Tbsp wheat germ |
| ½ | tsp salt |
| ½ | tsp baking soda |
| 3 | tsp baking powder |
| 1 | cup light brown sugar |
| 1½ | tsp grated lemon peel |
| 4 | Tbsp firm butter |
| 1 | cup walnuts, broken up |
| ⅓ | cup lemon juice (about 2 small lemons) |
| ⅔ | cup water |
| 2 | eggs, slightly beaten |

Preheat oven to 350°.

In medium-size bowl combine 1¼ cups whole wheat flour, 1¼ cups white flour, ¼ cup soy flour, 2 Tbsp wheat germ, ½ tsp salt, ½ tsp baking soda, 3 tsp baking powder, 1 cup light brown sugar with lumps broken up, and 1½ tsp grated lemon peel. Cut 4 Tbsp firm butter into mixture with knife, pastry blender, or tips of fingers until it looks like coarse crumbs. Add 1 cup broken walnuts and stir.

Stir ⅓ cup lemon juice into ⅔ cup water. Slightly beat 2 eggs and add with lemon water to dry ingredients. Stir and beat mixture with wooden spoon until all ingredients are moistened and batter forms.

Spoon batter into 1 greased large bread pan, filling pan ½–¾ full. (Or use 1 small pan and 2 mini pans.)

Place in preheated 350° oven and bake 1¼ hours for large loaf or 1 hour for smaller loaves, or until done when tested with cake tester.

Remove bread from oven and *let cool in pans* about 10 minutes before removing to rack to finish cooling.


## SALTLESS BROWN-RICE RAISIN BREAD

*Makes 1 loaf.* Despite being saltless, this is good either plain or buttered.

|       |                       |
|-------|-----------------------|
| ⅓     | cup milk, scalded     |
| 2     | eggs, slightly beaten |
| ½     | cup honey             |
| ¼     | cup peanut oil        |
| 1½    | cups brown rice flour |
| ½     | cup soy flour         |
| 2     | Tbsp wheat germ       |
| ½     | tsp baking soda       |
| 1     | Tbsp baking powder    |

<pre>
½    cup raisins
¼    cup nuts chopped, unsalted and unroasted
         (almonds are very nice)
</pre>

Preheat oven to 350°.

Scald ⅓ cup milk in saucepan and cool to body temperature.

Combine 2 slightly beaten eggs, ½ cup honey, and ¼ cup peanut oil. When milk has cooled sufficiently, add to eggs-honey-oil solution.

In large bowl mix together 1½ cups brown rice flour, ½ cup soy flour, 2 Tbsp wheat germ, ½ tsp baking soda, 1 Tbsp baking powder, ½ cup raisins, and ¼ cup chopped nuts.

Pour liquid ingredients into dry all at once and mix well. Spoon into greased medium-size bread pan and let stand for 1 hour. Bake in preheated 350° oven for about 1 hour or until cake tester comes out clean when inserted into bread.

## AMERICANA STEAMED BROWN BREAD

*Makes 2 loaves.* In almost every Early American recipe book, you come across a recipe for brown bread—a dark, moist, slightly sweet bread cooked by steaming rather than baking. Here is another, steamed in coffee cans.

<pre>
 1     cup chopped Calmyrna figs (white figs)
 ¾     cup orange juice
 1     cup cornmeal
 1     cup wheat germ or bran
1½     tsp salt
1½     tsp baking soda
 1     cup black raisins
 1     cup white or yellow raisins
1½     cups buttermilk
 ½     cup molasses
</pre>

In bowl soak 1 cup chopped figs in ¾ cup orange juice 30 minutes.

In another bowl blend 1 cup cornmeal, 1 cup wheat germ or bran, 1½ tsp salt, and 1½ tsp baking soda.

Drain figs (doing whatever you want with juice). Add figs, 1 cup black raisins, and 1 cup white or yellow raisins to dry ingredients, mixing until thoroughly dredged in flour. Mix in 1½ cups buttermilk and ½ cup molasses.

Grease inside surfaces of 2 clean 1-pound coffee cans. Divide mixture between these cans. Double a sheet of aluminum foil and fasten it over top of each can with rubber band (foil should reach down to middle of can).

Place cans in large pot. Add enough water to pot so that water comes halfway up cans. Put lid on pot. Place pot on burner of stove and let water in pot boil for 3 hours (replenishing water supply when necessary to maintain level halfway up cans).

Remove cans from water. Take off foil. Heat oven to 350°. Place open cans in oven 10 minutes.

Remove cans from oven. Let them cool for 15 minutes so that bread comes away from sides of can. Remove bread from cans. (If it does not come out easily, cut out bottom of can and push bread through.) Store in foil or plastic and refrigerate or freeze. Serve cold, warmed to room temperature, or toasted.

## RICH IRISH BREAD

*Makes 1 loaf.* This recipe was derived from one given by an Irish friend of Diana's, Catherine Condon. The bread can also be made without baking powder, eggs, or raisins. Catherine also suggests using the same recipe to make Irish Scones.

| | |
|---:|:---|
| 3 | cups unsifted unbleached white flour |
| ¼ | cup light brown sugar |
| 1 | tsp salt |
| 1 | Tbsp baking powder |
| 1 | tsp baking soda |
| 4 | Tbsp firm butter |
| ¾–1 | cup raisins |
| 2 | eggs, slightly beaten |
| 1–1¼ | cups buttermilk |

Preheat oven to 350°.

Place 3 cups white flour in large bowl, adding ¼ cup light brown sugar with lumps broken up, 1 tsp salt, 1 Tbsp baking powder, and 1 tsp baking soda. Cut 4 Tbsp firm butter into flour mixture with knife, pastry blender, or tips of fingers until it looks like coarse crumbs.

Add raisins and mix up with fingertips so that air gets into mixture.

Combine 2 slightly beaten eggs and 1 cup buttermilk. Pour into dry ingredients and mix until you have soft, loose dough. Add more buttermilk as needed to gain this consistency. Turn out onto floured board and knead about 10 times.

Shape dough into round or oblong loaf. Place in 10-inch round greased pan or pie plate, or in medium-size loaf pan. With sharp knife slash oblong loaf or make cross on round loaf about ½ inch deep.

Bake in preheated 350° oven for about 1 hour or until cake tester or toothpick inserted in center comes out clean.

Remove bread from pan and place on rack to cool. Or serve hot out of the oven with butter—delightful.

*Note:* Bread can be made with approximately 2 cups sweet milk instead of buttermilk; but then omit baking soda and increase amount of baking powder by 1 teaspoon.

---

# IRISH BROWN BREAD

*Makes 1 large loaf or 2 small loaves.* Tastes a little like yeast bread, though it's firmer, with a fine texture. Marvelous warm but good cold too, if you can wait that long.

|       |                           |
|------:|---------------------------|
| 4     | cups whole wheat flour    |
| 2     | cups unbleached white flour |
| 1/3   | cup brown sugar           |
| 2     | tsp baking soda           |
| 2     | tsp salt                  |
| 1/3   | cup firm butter           |
| 1     | cup raisins (optional)    |
| 2     | eggs, slightly beaten     |
| 1¾–2  | cups buttermilk           |

Preheat oven to 425°.

In medium-size mixing bowl combine 4 cups whole wheat flour, 2 cups white flour, 1/3 cup brown sugar with lumps broken up, 2 tsp baking soda, and 2 tsp salt. Mix well.

With tips of fingers or pastry blender rub in 1/3 cup firm butter until mixture has consistency of coarse crumbs. Add raisins and mix up with fingertips. This allows air to get into mixture.

Make well in center of mixture and put in 2 eggs, slightly beaten. Add about 1¾ cups buttermilk and beat mixture with wooden spoon. Add more buttermilk as needed. You may need more or less liquid, depending on absorbent quality of flours. Dough should be soft but manageable.

When dough starts to leave sides of bowl, turn out onto bread board and knead about 15 times. Leave dough in one piece, form into ball, flatten out in circle with palm of your hand to about 1–1½ inches thick for large single loaf. It is also possible to form 2 oblong or 2 round loaves.

With sharp knife slash center of round loaf or loaves ½ inch deep, crisscross; or make 1 slash on oblong loaves from end to end.

Place loaves in ungreased pie plates, soufflé dishes, or on

baking sheet and bake in preheated 425° oven for 30 minutes. Then turn oven down to 350° and bake for additional 20 minutes. If you are baking 1 large loaf, bake at 425° for 30 minutes and at 350° for 30–45 minutes and test with cake tester or toothpick to make sure it is done.

## SALT-FREE NUT SPOON BREAD

*Serves 4.* This makes a porridge-like soft bread food for serving in place of rice, potatoes, or noodles.

|     |     |
| --- | --- |
| 1   | cup cornmeal |
| 1   | cup water |
| 1½  | cups scalded milk |
| ½   | cup sweet butter |
| 1   | beaten egg |
| 2   | Tbsp sunflower seeds (shelled) |
| 2   | Tbsp pumpkin seeds (shelled) |

Preheat oven to 350°.

In saucepan mix 1 cup cornmeal into 1 cup water. Bring to boil and cook over low heat 10 minutes, stirring to prevent burning.

In second pot scald 1½ cups milk. Melt ½ cup butter into it and stir this, a little at a time, into your first saucepan. Quickly stir in 1 beaten egg. Mix in 2 Tbsp sunflower seeds and 2 Tbsp pumpkin seeds.

Pour into oiled large glass pie plate, casserole, or square pan. Bake in preheated 350° oven for 35–40 minutes. Serve hot in baking pan.

# Popovers

# WHITE AND SOY POPOVERS

*Makes about 6 large popovers.* The drama of the popover is the transformation of thin batter into a large, hollow, crusty shell. Steam trapped inside the quick-forming crust causes this magical change—it can only happen in a rather hot oven. Fantastic treat with creamy butter.

|       |                                   |
|-------|-----------------------------------|
| 1     | Tbsp melted butter                |
| 3/4   | cup sifted unbleached white flour |
| 1     | tsp salt                          |
| 1/4   | cup soy flour                     |
| 1     | cup milk                          |
| 2     | eggs                              |

Preheat oven to 425°. Preheat popover pan or custard cups. Melt 1 Tbsp butter for greasing pan. Set aside.

Sift together 3/4 cup white flour and 1 tsp salt. Stir in 1/4 cup soy flour.

Using blender or rotary beater combine flour mixture with 1 cup milk and 2 eggs, blending or beating until light and airy. Using pastry brush, grease preheated popover pan, muffin pan, or ovenware glass custard cups *very lightly* with melted butter. Fill cups 1/2 full with batter and carefully place in preheated oven. Bake at 425° for approximately 30 minutes or until golden brown. *Don't peek at these until last 5 minutes, as they rise from steam and fall easily!* If middle is not completely risen, they should be baked longer. Try baking next batch for 40–45 minutes at slightly lower temperature.

---

# WHOLE WHEAT POPOVERS

*Makes 6 large or 12 medium popovers.* Since whole wheat flour rises less readily than white flour, these are less airy, a little thicker and coarser than the preceding popovers. Nice hot, plain or with butter, for sturdier tastes.

|   | |
|---|---|
| 1 | Tbsp melted butter |
| ¼ | cup unsifted unbleached white flour |
| About ¾ | cup whole wheat flour |
| 1 | tsp salt |
| 1 | tsp brown sugar or molasses |
| 3 | eggs |
| 1 | cup milk |

Preheat oven to 500°. Also preheat popover pan.

Melt 1 Tbsp butter for greasing pan. Set aside.

In 1-cup measure put ¼ cup white flour and fill measure to 1-cup mark with whole wheat flour. Pour into medium-size bowl. Add 1 tsp salt and 1 tsp brown sugar with lumps broken up and mix well. (If using molasses, mix with eggs and milk.)

In separate container beat together with electric blender or rotary beater 3 eggs and 1 cup milk.

Add to flour mixture and beat with beater or blender.

Using pastry brush, lightly grease preheated popover pan, muffin pan, or ovenware glass custard cups with melted butter.

Fill cups ½ full with batter and carefully place in preheated 500° oven. Bake for 10 minutes, then lower temperature to a little less than 400° for additional 20 minutes. *Do not peek at these until last 5 minutes.* If they fall they have not been baked long enough.

# Muffins

# MUFFIN-MAKING MEMO

Read through the recipe, assembling all required ingredients (or suitable substitutes) and equipment.

1. Turn the oven on to the required temperature—most likely hot as muffins are "quick breads."

2. Grease cups of muffin pan lightly (or as directed) and place pan in oven to warm.

3. Measure out flour. If using unbleached white, sift it for an accurate measurement. Place premeasured flour and other dry ingredients into mixing bowl.

4. If using firm shortening—butter or margarine—measure out and cut in with pastry blender, knife, fork, or fingertips. If a slightly beaten egg is used, blend it with liquid.

If using oil, measure and combine it with egg or other liquid ingredients used.

5. Pour liquid ingredients into flour mixture all at once. Stir only until flour mixture is moistened. The batter can be lumpy.

6. Remove muffin pan from oven. If you are concerned about sticking, sprinkle a little flour on the bottom of each cup. Fill cups ½, ⅔, or ¾ full, according to recipe.

7. Bake muffins to a golden brown, 20–30 minutes or longer.

8. Remove from pan and serve immediately.

Some muffins are just as good cold or reheated (you can check this in the recipe).

# FANTASTIC BLUEBERRY MUFFINS

*Makes 12 large muffins.* Naturally these taste best if you picked the blueberries yourself, but don't wait until summer to try them, or you'll be missing a fantastic taste experience.

|      |                                         |
| ---- | --------------------------------------- |
| 2    | Tbsp wheat germ                         |
| 2    | cups sifted unbleached white flour      |
| 3    | tsp baking powder                       |
| ¾    | tsp salt                                |
| ½    | cup light brown sugar (if using         |
|      | canned blueberries, reduce sugar to ¼ cup) |
| 1    | egg, beaten                             |
| ⅔    | cup milk                                |
| ⅓    | cup corn oil                            |
| ¾–1  | cup fresh or frozen whole blueberries   |
|      | (thawed and drained),                   |
|      | or ½ cup canned (drained)               |

Preheat oven to 425°.

Grease cups of muffin pan and mini loaf pan.

Into medium-size mixing bowl put 2 Tbsp wheat germ. Sift in 2 cups white flour, 3 tsp baking powder, and ¾ tsp salt. Stir. Add ½ (or ¼) cup light brown sugar with lumps broken up and stir thoroughly. Add 1 beaten egg, ⅔ cup milk, and ⅓ cup corn oil and stir only enough to make moist, lumpy batter.

Wash and drain ¾–1 cup fresh blueberries; or thaw and drain ¾–1 cup frozen blueberries; or drain (do not rinse) ½ cup canned blueberries. Fold blueberries into batter.

Spoon mixture into muffin cups ½–⅔ full. If you have extra batter, spoon into mini loaf pan, up to ½ full. Bake 18–24 minutes or until light brown on edges. Mini loaf will take a little longer.

# SWEET MUFFINS

*Makes 8 large or 12 medium muffins.* They are plain and they are good.

|        |                                    |
|--------|------------------------------------|
| 1½     | cups sifted unbleached white flour |
| 2      | tsp baking powder                  |
| 1      | tsp salt                           |
| 2      | Tbsp wheat germ                    |
| 2      | Tbsp soy flour                     |
| 3      | Tbsp light brown sugar             |
| 1      | egg, slightly beaten               |
| 1      | cup milk                           |
| 4      | Tbsp melted butter or oil          |

Preheat oven to 385°.

Into medium-size bowl sift together 1½ cups flour, 2 tsp baking powder, and 1 tsp salt. Add 2 Tbsp wheat germ, 2 Tbsp soy flour, and 3 Tbsp light brown sugar with lumps broken up. Stir well.

In second container slightly beat 1 egg and add 1 cup milk and 4 Tbsp melted butter or oil. Beat until light and foamy.

Add liquid to dry ingredients all at once and stir just until flour is moistened. Batter can be somewhat lumpy.

Fill greased cups of muffin pan about ⅔–¾ full and bake at 385° for about 30 minutes or until done when tested with cake tester.

Serve hot or cold.

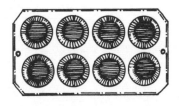

---

*Quick Breads*

# DIANA'S FAVORITE CORN MUFFINS

*Makes 12 large muffins.* Best eaten with butter, straight from the oven, but very good reheated too.

|       |                                        |
|-------|----------------------------------------|
| 1     | egg, beaten                            |
| 1     | cup milk                               |
| 3     | Tbsp light brown sugar                 |
| 3     | Tbsp corn oil                          |
| 1     | cup whole grain yellow or white cornmeal |
| 1     | cup sifted unbleached white flour      |
| 1     | Tbsp wheat germ                        |
| ½     | tsp salt                               |
| 3     | tsp baking powder                      |

Preheat oven to 450°.

In mixing bowl beat 1 egg, then beat in 1 cup milk, 3 Tbsp light brown sugar with lumps broken up, and 3 Tbsp corn oil.

In separate bowl mix 1 cup cornmeal, 1 cup white flour, 1 Tbsp wheat germ, ½ tsp salt, and 3 tsp baking powder.

Grease cups of muffin pan with corn oil, generously, and put in oven to warm.

Add dry ingredients to liquid and mix quickly with 4 or 5 stirring strokes with fork.

Take hot muffin pan out of oven and spoon in mixture, filling each cup of muffin pan ½–¾ full.

Put in oven, turning temperature control down to 425°, and bake for 20 minutes or until golden brown around edges.

# HEARTY CORNMEAL AND WHEAT MUFFINS

*Makes 8 large or 12 medium-size muffins.* These muffins are great for quick energy and staying power. When you make them for breakfast, save a few for extra nourishment during the day. Excellent plain, good with butter too.

½ cup cornmeal
½ cup whole wheat flour
¼ cup wheat germ
¼ cup soy flour
2 tsp baking powder
1 tsp salt
1 egg, slightly beaten
¾ cup milk
¼ cup maple syrup, molasses, honey,
   or brown sugar
¼ cup corn oil

Preheat oven to 450°. Grease cups of muffin pan with corn oil or butter.

In medium-size mixing bowl combine ½ cup cornmeal, ½ cup whole wheat flour, ¼ cup wheat germ, and ¼ cup soy flour. Add 2 tsp baking powder and 1 tsp salt and mix well.

In separate bowl beat together 1 egg, ¾ cup milk, ¼ cup sweetening (maple syrup, molasses, honey, or brown sugar), and ¼ cup corn oil.

Put well-greased muffin pan in oven for a couple of minutes while combining dry and liquid ingredients all at once in medium-size mixing bowl. Stir together quickly, only as much as necessary to wet all dry ingredients.

Take hot muffin pan from oven and fill muffin cups ½–⅔ full. Bake 15–20 minutes in 450° oven. Eat hot or cold.

# CHEWY WHOLE WHEAT MUFFINS

*Makes 12 large muffins.* Substantial and satisfying. Eat while hot, and save extras for snacks.

          1   cup sifted whole wheat flour
          ¾   cup sifted unbleached white flour
          2   Tbsp soy flour
          3   tsp baking powder
          1   tsp salt
          1   Tbsp wheat germ
          1   Tbsp brewer's yeast
          ¼   cup light brown sugar
          4   Tbsp firm butter
          1   egg, slightly beaten
          1   cup milk
              Cornmeal

Preheat oven to 450°.

Into 2-cup measure sift whole wheat flour to 1-cup mark. On top of it sift in white flour to 1¾-cup mark; then put in 2 Tbsp soy flour, 3 tsp baking powder, and 1 tsp salt. Pour into medium-size mixing bowl and add 1 Tbsp wheat germ, 1 Tbsp brewer's yeast, and ¼ cup light brown sugar with lumps broken up. Mix well.

Grease cups of muffin pan with butter and sprinkle bottoms with cornmeal. Put muffin pan in oven to warm while completing muffin batter.

Cut 4 Tbsp firm butter into pieces over dry ingredients, then rub in or cut in until mixture has texture of coarse crumbs.

Mix in 1 slightly beaten egg and 1 cup milk, stirring only until all dry ingredients are moistened.

Take hot muffin pan from oven and fill muffin cups ½–⅔ full. Return to oven and bake 20 minutes or until muffins are rich medium brown.

---

# WHEAT GERM MUFFINS

*Makes 12 large muffins.* These fragrant muffins are best while still hot. They are filling and sustaining.

> 1 cup whole wheat flour
> 1 cup wheat germ
> ½ tsp baking soda
> 1 tsp salt
> ¼ cup (or more) raisins
> 2 eggs, separated
> 3 Tbsp melted butter
> ¼ cup molasses
> 1 cup buttermilk

Preheat oven to 400°.

In medium bowl mix well 1 cup whole wheat flour, 1 cup wheat germ, ½ tsp baking soda, 1 tsp salt, and ¼ cup raisins. Set aside.

Separate whites and yolks of 2 eggs. Into container with yolks beat 3 Tbsp melted butter, ¼ cup molasses, and 1 cup buttermilk. Set aside.

Beat egg whites in their container until stiff. Set aside.

Put well-greased muffin pan into oven to warm.

Pour egg yolk mixture into dry ingredients and stir until moist. Fold in egg whites.

Take muffin pan from oven and fill muffin cups ⅔–¾ full, without smoothing tops of muffins. If there is excess batter put it in greased mini loaf pan.

Bake for 20 minutes, or until toothpick or cake tester inserted into muffin comes out clean. Mini loaf will take a little longer.

Remove immediately from pan(s) and serve while still hot. Good plain, or with butter or honey.

# OATMEAL MUFFINS

*Makes 8 large or 12 medium muffins.* They're moist and rich.

        1   cup rolled oats
        1   cup buttermilk
        5   Tbsp brown sugar
        ⅓   cup softened butter
        1   egg
        1   cup sifted unbleached white flour
        1   tsp baking powder
        ½   tsp baking soda
        1   tsp salt
        1   Tbsp wheat germ

Soak 1 cup rolled oats in 1 cup buttermilk 15–45 minutes, depending upon your time and how quickly oats absorb buttermilk.

Preheat oven to 375°–400°.

In large bowl combine 5 Tbsp brown sugar with lumps broken up, ⅓ cup softened butter, and 1 egg, blending until creamy.

Into medium-size bowl sift 1 cup flour, 1 tsp baking powder, ½ tsp baking soda, and 1 tsp salt. Add 1 Tbsp wheat germ and mix.

Add dry ingredients alternately with oats and buttermilk to shortening mixture. Stir until just dampened and fill greased cups of muffin pan about ⅔–¾ full. Bake at 375°–400° about 45 minutes or longer or until golden brown.

Remove from pan and serve immediately.

# BROWN RICE AND SOY FLOUR MUFFINS

*Makes 12 large muffins.* These cake-like muffins are delicious when hot or warm, but not nearly as good cold.

         1½    cups brown rice flour
         ½     cup soy flour
         1     tsp baking soda
         1     tsp salt
         2     Tbsp brown sugar
         2     eggs, beaten slightly
         3     Tbsp oil
         2     cups buttermilk

Preheat oven to 450°.

In medium-size bowl sift together 1½ cups brown rice flour, ½ cup soy flour, 1 tsp baking soda, and 1 tsp salt. Add 2 Tbsp brown sugar with lumps broken up, and mix well.

Grease 12-cup muffin pan or small muffin pan and mini loaf pan, and put in oven to warm.

Beat 2 eggs slightly in another bowl, then beat in 3 Tbsp oil, and 2 cups buttermilk.

Add liquid ingredients all at once to dry mixture and stir together with fork until barely mixed, being careful not to overmix. Take pan(s) from oven and fill cups ⅔ full, without smoothing tops.

Bake 15–20 minutes in 450° oven.

Remove from pan(s) and serve immediately.

# BRAN, RAISIN, AND NUT MUFFINS

*Makes 12 large muffins.* Chewy muffins are best eaten hot, but are also good later in the day for snacks.

1 cup bran
1 cup sifted unbleached white flour
1 tsp salt
½ tsp baking soda
1 Tbsp wheat germ
1 Tbsp brewer's yeast
⅓ cup brown sugar
¼ cup raisins
¼ cup chopped nuts
1 cup buttermilk

Preheat oven to 350°.

In medium bowl mix 1 cup bran, 1 cup white flour, 1 tsp salt, ½ tsp baking soda, 1 Tbsp wheat germ, 1 Tbsp brewer's yeast, ⅓ cup brown sugar with lumps broken up, ¼ cup raisins, and ¼ cup chopped nuts. Stir well.

Grease large 12-cup muffin pan, or small muffin pan and mini loaf pan, and put in preheated oven to warm.

Pour 1 cup buttermilk into dry ingredients and mix with fork just until all dry ingredients are moistened.

Take pan(s) from oven and fill each cup ⅔–¾ full (do not smooth tops of muffins); mini pan up to ½ full.

Return to oven and bake 20–30 minutes, or until muffins begin to brown. Bake mini pans a little longer.

Turn out of pan(s) and serve immediately.

# *Biscuits and Scones*

# BISCUIT TIPS

1. Turn on your oven, preheating it to suggested temperature. Read through the recipe, assembling necessary ingredients and utensils.

2. Sift flour, as suggested, and measure salt, baking powder, or soda into sifter. It is not necessary to sift whole wheat, rye, soy, oat, etc., flour. Combine dry ingredients in large mixing bowl.

3. Measure solid shortening and cut in with fork, knife, pastry blender, or fingertips until mixture has texture of coarse crumbs.

4. Turn dough out onto slightly floured surface. Knead lightly 5 or 6 times with fingertips (too much handling makes biscuits tough).

5. Roll or pat dough out to $\frac{1}{4}$ inch for thin, crusty biscuits or $\frac{1}{2}$–$\frac{3}{4}$ inch for thick soft biscuits. Cut in rounds with floured biscuit cutter or in squares with knife, pressing straight down in one stroke. Twisting or sawing with cutter or knife prevents biscuit's edges from rising properly. Gather together leftover dough. Pat out (don't knead) and cut.

6. On ungreased baking sheet place biscuits close together (for soft sides) or 1 inch apart (crusty sides). If you use a pan with sides, turn it upside down and bake biscuits on the bottom.

7. Bake biscuits in middle of oven until golden brown around edges.

## MAKING YOUR OWN BISCUIT
## OR ENGLISH MUFFIN CUTTER

Biscuit cutters can be made in various sizes—2¼-inch, 2½-inch, 3-inch, etc. Choose a can the size you want your biscuits or English muffins to be. A 4-inch-diameter can is good for English muffins.

Get out a roller-type can opener—one with a round cutting blade. Carefully cut out one end of can as smoothly as possible. This will be the end you use to cut dough. Empty and wash can.

On the other end of can make 2 cuts around the edge (like crescent moons or parentheses) leaving ½–¾ inch uncut on each side. Push the 2 cut edges together inside the can. The uncut strip in the middle makes the handle for your cutter.

# BASIC BISCUITS

*Makes 12–16 biscuits.* While it is alleged that in several Southern states serving reheated biscuits is a recognized ground for divorce, biscuits can be reheated later in the day for another meal—but they're not as good as when fresh from the oven. Very hungry children have been known to eat cold biscuits.

|          |                                     |
|----------|-------------------------------------|
| 2        | Tbsp wheat germ                     |
| 2        | Tbsp soy flour or soy powder        |
| 3        | tsp baking powder                   |
| 1        | tsp salt                            |
| Almost 2 | cups sifted unbleached white flour  |
| 5        | Tbsp firm butter                    |
| ¾        | cup milk                            |

Preheat oven to 450°.

In bottom of 2-cup measure put 2 Tbsp wheat germ. Sift in 2 Tbsp soy flour or powder, 3 tsp baking powder, 1 tsp salt, and enough white flour to fill measure. Place these dry ingredients in mixing bowl and stir together thoroughly.

Dot top of dry mixture with 5 Tbsp firm butter. With tips of fingers or pastry blender thoroughly cut butter into flour until mixture has texture of coarse sand.

Make well in center of mixture and pour in most of ¾ cup milk. Mix quickly with fork to form soft dough, adding remaining milk as necessary to achieve light but not very sticky dough. Mix just as much as necessary.

Turn out onto floured board or countertop and knead gently several times by folding dough in half and pressing lightly together.

Roll or pat dough ½–¾ inch thick and cut out biscuits with floured biscuit cutter. Place biscuits on ungreased baking sheet or upside-down baking pan, and bake in preheated 450° oven for 11–12 minutes, or until edges turn light brown.

Serve biscuits hot with butter, jam, molasses, or cooked fruit.

# SOUR CREAM BISCUITS

*Makes about 15 2-inch biscuits.* These biscuits have wonderful flavor and lightness.

|      |                                  |
|------|----------------------------------|
| 2    | Tbsp wheat germ                  |
| 2    | Tbsp soy flour or soy powder     |
| 2    | tsp baking powder                |
| ¼    | tsp baking soda                  |
| 1    | tsp salt                         |
| Almost 2 | cups sifted unbleached white flour |
| 4    | Tbsp firm butter                 |
| 1    | cup dairy sour cream             |

Preheat oven to 450°.

In bottom of 2-cup measure put 2 Tbsp wheat germ. Then sift into measure 2 Tbsp soy flour or powder, 2 tsp baking powder, ¼ tsp baking soda, 1 tsp salt, and enough white flour to fill measure. Pour into large bowl and mix well.

Blend in 4 Tbsp firm butter with pastry blender, fork, or tips of fingers until mixture resembles coarse crumbs.

Add 1 cup dairy sour cream and stir with fork until dough ball is barely formed, stirring as little as possible.

Turn onto lightly floured board, knead a few times, and roll or pat out ½–¾ inch thick. With large sharp knife cut into 2 inch or 3-inch squares by pressing knife straight down in 1 stroke for each cut. If you prefer, cut biscuits in round shape with biscuit cutter.

Place biscuits on ungreased baking sheet and bake at 450° until light brown on edges, usually about 10–20 minutes, depending upon thickness.

If you find yours not as light as you prefer, add 1 teaspoon more baking powder and ¼ teaspoon more baking soda next time you try this recipe.

# WASHINGTON'S ANGEL BISCUITS

*Makes about 12 biscuits.* These delicious biscuits have 3 methods of rising built in: yeast, baking powder, and the buttermilk-soda combination. They have a melt-in-the-mouth flavor, somewhere between straight baking powder biscuits and English muffins.

| | |
|---:|:---|
| 1 | Tbsp or pkg dry yeast |
| 3 | Tbsp water, body temperature |
| ¼ | cup wheat germ |
| ¼ | cup light brown sugar |
| ¼ | cup soy flour |
| 2½ | tsp baking powder |
| 1 | tsp salt |
| ½ | tsp baking soda |
| 2 | cups sifted unbleached white flour |
| ½ | cup firm butter |
| Almost 1 | cup buttermilk |

Preheat oven to 400°. Grease baking sheet.

Sprinkle 1 Tbsp or pkg dry yeast over 3 Tbsp water, body temperature. Stir and set aside.

Put ¼ cup wheat germ and ¼ cup light brown sugar with lumps broken up in bowl. Sift in ¼ cup soy flour, 2½ tsp baking powder, 1 tsp salt, and ½ tsp baking soda. Add 2 cups white flour and mix well.

Dot with ½ cup firm butter and blend or cut in until mixture looks like coarse crumbs.

Add yeast mixture and up to almost 1 cup buttermilk, to make barely moist dough, stirring in with fork until no flour is visible.

Turn out onto well-floured board and knead a few times to make smooth dough. Roll or pat out until half the desired thickness of finished biscuits (about ½–¾ inch thick usually). Cut out biscuits with floured cutter and place on greased baking sheet. If desired, brush tops with melted butter. Bake 15–20 minutes, until golden, and eat hot or cold.

If you want fewer biscuits, divide dough in half before baking and keep half of dough in refrigerator, in plastic bag or tightly covered. Be sure to use within 1 week. Before using dough, bring to room temperature.

## DROP BISCUITS

*Makes about 12 biscuits.* Drop biscuits take on their own unique, irregular shape. They should be eaten while hot, either plain, which is delicious, or with butter, applesauce, jam, honey, or molasses.

|   |   |
|---|---|
| 2 | Tbsp wheat germ |
| 2 | Tbsp soy flour or soy powder |
| 3 | tsp baking powder |
| 1 | tsp salt |
| Almost 2 | cups sifted unbleached white flour |
| ⅔ | cup milk |
| ⅓ | cup corn oil |

Preheat oven to 450°.

In bottom of 2-cup measure put 2 Tbsp wheat germ and 2 Tbsp soy flour or soy powder. Sift in 3 tsp baking powder and 1 tsp salt; then sift in sufficient white flour to fill measure. Pour into mixing bowl and mix thoroughly with fork.

Make a well in mixture and add ⅔ cup milk and ⅓ cup corn oil. Stir together with fork until dough forms loose ball which separates from sides of bowl. Be careful not to overmix.

Using soup spoon or tablespoon, drop spoonfuls of dough on ungreased baking sheet, leaving ½ inch between drops. Gauge size of drops so that you get about 12 and don't worry about their irregular appearance.

Bake 11–12 minutes or until light brown on edges, or characteristic biscuit color.

For variation substitute some sifted whole wheat flour for part of white flour.

## WHOLE WHEAT
## FINGERTIP BISCUITS

*Makes 9 or 10 biscuits.* Nourishes you until the next meal.

    1   cup unsifted whole wheat pastry flour
    1   tsp salt
    1   rounded tsp baking powder
    5   Tbsp firm butter
    1   beaten egg
    1   Tbsp honey
        Small amount of milk

Preheat oven to 450°.

Place 1 cup whole wheat pastry flour in mixing bowl and add 1 tsp salt and 1 rounded tsp baking powder. Stir together, then cut or blend in 5 Tbsp firm butter broken into small pieces, until mixture has texture of coarse crumbs.

In measuring cup break and beat 1 egg. Add 1 Tbsp honey, and enough milk to fill to $\frac{1}{2}$-cup mark. Stir together.

Add liquid ingredients to dry and stir with fork until barely mixed.

Using large soup spoon or small serving spoon, put 9 or 10 piles of dough on ungreased baking sheet. With fingertips gently shape each small pile into casually rounded biscuit.

Bake in 450° oven for 12 minutes, or until edges begin to brown.

# CORNMEAL BISCUITS

*Makes about 12 biscuits.* These biscuits have an agreeable heartiness.

|        |                                    |
|-------:|------------------------------------|
| ¾      | cup cornmeal                       |
| 1¼     | cups sifted unbleached white flour |
| 3      | tsp baking powder                  |
| 1      | tsp salt                           |
| 2      | Tbsp wheat germ                    |
| 4      | Tbsp firm butter                   |
| About ¾ | cup milk                          |

Preheat oven to 450°.

Sift into bowl ¾ cup cornmeal, 1¼ cups flour, 3 tsp baking powder, and 1 tsp salt. Add 2 Tbsp wheat germ and stir together.

Cut or blend in 4 Tbsp firm butter until texture of mixture resembles coarse meal.

Stir in about ¾ cup milk, sufficient to make soft dough, and turn out onto lightly floured bread board.

Knead 7 or 8 times, then pat out or roll to ¾-inch thickness. Cut out biscuits with cutter and place on ungreased baking sheet. If desired, brush tops with melted butter.

Bake 9–10 minutes in preheated hot oven, or until brown on edges.

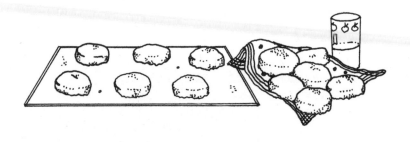

# CREAM SCONES

*Makes 8 scones.* Scones closely resemble biscuits but are much more solid. Wonderful with butter, honey, and jam. Traditionally served for afternoon tea but great anytime.

|       |                                    |
|-------|------------------------------------|
| 2     | cups unsifted unbleached white flour |
| ½     | tsp baking powder                  |
| 1     | Tbsp light brown sugar             |
| 1     | tsp salt                           |
| 4     | Tbsp firm butter                   |
| ½     | cup heavy cream                    |

Preheat oven to 400°.

In large bowl combine 2 cups white flour, ½ tsp baking powder, 1 Tbsp light brown sugar with lumps broken up, and 1 tsp salt. With pastry blender, fork, or tips of fingers rub or cut in 4 Tbsp firm butter until mixture has consistency of coarse crumbs. Stir in ½ cup heavy cream. Dough should be stiff but add additional cream if necessary, as it should not be too crumbly.

Turn out onto board and knead until dough sticks together. Divide dough in half. Form ball and press or roll dough out in circle about 1 inch thick. With sharp knife cut circle into quarters and arrange pieces on ungreased baking sheet about 1 inch apart. Repeat with second half of dough. Brush tops with melted butter.

Bake in preheated 400° oven for 35–40 minutes or until light brown (biscuit color). Serve hot.

# Pancakes

# KEEP YOUR GRIDDLE IN GOOD TEMPER

A cast-iron griddle that fits over two burners of your stove will make pancake baking a lot easier. If you get one, follow the manufacturer's directions for initially cleaning and tempering it. When using, heat it slowly; best to start before mixing your ingredients, or as the recipe directs. It's ready when a drop of water dances on it, rather than evaporating immediately (too hot), or spreading out (too cold). After testing, adjust heat if necessary. When griddle is hot enough, lower heat to maintain even temperature.

A little butter or peanut oil, used sparingly, will clean your griddle after using. Don't wash it except in emergencies; if you do, then temper it again before using to prevent sticking.

If you don't have a griddle, use one or two skillets. Lightly grease with butter or peanut oil and determine the right temperature as you would for a cast-iron griddle.

If you have electric fry pan, follow manufacturer's directions for baking pancakes.

# CONTINENTAL PANCAKES

*Makes about 24 pancakes.* These thin pancakes are basically the same throughout Europe, though the people in one country may prefer them a little thinner, or may substitute sugar for salt or vice versa. Often, the pancakes are rolled around a stuffing of one kind or another; or they are not stuffed, but served flat with a little liqueur. What is also nice is that you can store part of the batter in the refrigerator to use a day or two later, if you can't eat any more. This batter can be made in advance. It's great to take along camping, so long as you keep it cool.

> 1 cup sifted unbleached white flour
> ½ tsp salt
> 2 eggs, slightly beaten
> 1 cup milk or ½ cup milk and ½ cup water
> 2 Tbsp melted butter

Place in large bowl 1 cup white flour and ½ tsp salt. Add 2 eggs, slightly beaten, and 1 cup milk or ½ cup milk and ½ cup water. Beat with wire whisk or rotary beater until smooth. Add 2 Tbsp melted butter and continue beating. If using blender, put in all ingredients and blend at top speed for 1 minute. Batter should be very light and thin.

Refrigerate until ready to use.

The pan used is very important in making these pancakes. A French crepe pan is perfect, but requirements are long handle, sloping sides, and a 6-inch to 7-inch base.

Melt a little butter in bottom of pan and place over moderate heat. Remove just before butter burns. Hold pan away from heat and pour into middle about 1 Tbsp less than ¼ cup of batter. Tilt pan so that batter runs all over bottom of pan and just coats it. There should be very little excess. If there is too much use less batter on next one. Return pan to heat and quickly fry pancake on one side and then other, which should take only a few seconds. (Pancake is ready to turn when you can jerk it loose from bottom.)

Crepes or pancakes themselves can be made in advance, stuffed, and reheated in oven, though they won't be as crisp. Stuff with apricot preserves and almonds, roll, and serve with sour cream; or stuff with applesauce, sprinkle with sugar and cinnamon, and roll. Most jams are good to use.

Or roll pancake, cut in slices, and serve like noodles in soup stock, plain or with chopped chives, etc. Kids, young and old, love it.

## MOTHER MEERWARTH'S GERMAN ONE-PANCAKE RECIPE OR, A DIFFERENT WAY TO EAT AN EGG

*Makes 1 large pancake.* Diana's mother used to make this in the morning for her father before he went to work. It is fast, quick, good, and another way to eat an egg. He always enjoyed it with applesauce and a little sugar and cinnamon.

> ¼    cup unsifted unbleached white flour or, as Mother says, 3 heaping tsp flour
>      Pinch of salt
> About ¼   cup milk
>    1    egg, slightly beaten

Heat large 10-inch skillet over moderate heat.

With rotary beater or in 1-cup shaker blend together ¼ cup flour, pinch of salt, about ¼ cup milk, and 1 slightly beaten egg.

Grease skillet with butter and pour in batter, tipping until batter is evenly distributed all over bottom of skillet. (If you are using smaller pan, make 2 pancakes!) Turn pancake as soon as it is puffed and full of bubbles. Brown on other side.

*To make 2 German-style pancakes:* Add ¼ cup more flour, increase salt to ¼ tsp, and add ¼ cup more milk.

---

# BLINI

*Makes about 20 blini, enough for 3 or 4 people.* These small pancakes are served with sour cream. If you want to use them as an appetizer, serve them on a tray with piles of grated onion, grated cheese, a sour cream pot, and saltcellar, and let your friends help themselves.

*Ingredients for first step:*

| | |
|---|---|
| ½ | cup water, body temperature |
| 1 | Tbsp or pkg dry yeast |
| ¼ | cup milk, body temperature |
| ½ | cup buckwheat flour |

*Ingredients used later:*

| | |
|---|---|
| ¾ | cup milk, body temperature |
| 1 | Tbsp melted butter |
| 1 | tsp light brown sugar |
| ½ | tsp salt |
| 2 | eggs, separated |
| ½ | cup buckwheat flour |

In medium-size bowl put ½ cup water, body temperature, and 1 Tbsp or pkg dry yeast. Stir and set aside.

Warm ¼ cup milk to body temperature and add to yeast mixture. Beat in ½ cup buckwheat flour.

Cover with towel and set in warm place until light and bubbly (2–3 hours); or if you want blini for breakfast, refrigerate overnight.

When mixture is light begin second phase. Warm ¾ cup milk to body temperature and melt 1 Tbsp butter in it. Add 1 tsp light brown sugar and ½ tsp salt. Stir. In large bowl beat 2 egg yolks. Gradually add warm milk-butter mixture, yeast–buckwheat flour mixture and ½ cup additional buckwheat flour. Beat into smooth batter.

Whip 2 egg whites until they form stiff peaks. Fold them into

blini batter, cover, and set aside for at least 30 minutes or more in warm place (75°–80°).

Heat griddle and just before using, brush with butter. With large spoon pour out small pancakes onto griddle, 2–3 inches wide. Bake until edges are brown; turn and brown on other side.

Put finished blinis in warm oven until all are done and serve on warm plate or platter.

## BAKING POWDER BUCKWHEAT PANCAKES

*Makes 8–10 medium pancakes.* Delicious, quick pancakes made with your favorite berries.

| | |
|---|---|
| ¼ | cup butter, melted |
| ½ | cup buckwheat flour |
| 6 | Tbsp whole wheat flour |
| 1½ | tsp baking powder |
| ½ | tsp salt |
| 1 | egg, separated |
| ¾–1 | cup milk |
| 2 | tsp molasses |
| ½ | cup blueberries or your favorite berries, drained |

If using heavy cast-iron griddle, preheat while preparing batter.

In saucepan melt ¼ cup butter. Set aside.

In medium-size container combine ½ cup buckwheat flour, 6 Tbsp whole wheat flour, 1½ tsp baking powder, and ½ tsp salt. Mix dry ingredients.

Separate 1 egg. Make a well in flour mixture and drop in egg yolk. Gradually add ¾–1 cup milk, 2 tsp molasses, and melted butter, blending in and beating mixture at same time.

In small container whip egg white until light and stiff. Fold into batter.

Just before you are ready to fry pancakes *gently* fold in ½ cup drained berries. Batter will take on color of berries.

From tip of large spoon pour batter onto ungreased griddle in pools a little apart. When pancakes start to puff and are full of bubbles, turn and brown on other side.


## OLD-FASHIONED BUCKWHEAT CAKES

*Makes about 15 medium pancakes.* These are very good with buckwheat honey.

|      |                                      |
|------|--------------------------------------|
| 1    | cup buckwheat flour                  |
| ½    | cup cornmeal                         |
| ½    | cup whole wheat flour or wheat germ  |
| 1    | Tbsp light brown sugar               |
| 1    | tsp salt                             |
| 1    | Tbsp or pkg dry yeast                |
| 1¾   | cups water, body temperature         |
| ½    | tsp baking soda                      |
| 2    | Tbsp melted butter                   |

The night before you want buckwheat cakes mix 1 cup buckwheat flour, ½ cup cornmeal, ½ cup whole wheat flour or wheat germ, 1 Tbsp light brown sugar with lumps broken up, and 1 tsp salt.

In separate mixing bowl sprinkle 1 Tbsp or pkg dry yeast over 1¾ cups water, body temperature. Stir with wooden spoon to soften yeast.

Add flour-meal mixture a little at a time, to make batter of pouring consistency. Cover and put in moderately warm place overnight.

In morning stir in ½ tsp baking soda and 2 Tbsp melted butter. Set aside while warming griddle.

Brush griddle lightly with butter and pour on small pools of batter for medium-size pancakes. Brown until edges are crisp and turn once to brown other side.

Eat with buckwheat honey, molasses, or syrup, and plenty of butter.


## RAISED BUCKWHEAT PANCAKES

*Makes about 15 medium pancakes.* Here are the simplest buckwheat cakes, greatly enjoyed in the past, and delicious in the present. A few go a long way toward filling the gap between getting up and lunch.

|   |   |
|---|---|
| 1¾ | cups water, body temperature |
| 1 | Tbsp or pkg dry yeast |
| 2 | cups buckwheat flour |
| 1 | tsp salt |
| ½ | tsp baking soda |
| ¼ | cup water, body temperature |
| 3–4 | Tbsp melted butter |

The night before you want buckwheat cakes pour 1¾ cups water, body temperature, into mixing bowl and sprinkle over it 1 Tbsp or pkg dry yeast.

Stir in up to 2 cups buckwheat flour a little at a time, until you have batter of pouring consistency. Add 1 tsp salt, cover, and set aside until morning in place which is 60°–70°; or if weather is hot, put in refrigerator overnight and take out in morning 30 minutes before using.

In morning put griddle over low heat and uncover batter. It will be light and bubbly. Mix ½ tsp baking soda with ¼ cup water, body temperature. Melt 3 or 4 Tbsp butter. Lightly grease griddle with a little butter and stir the rest, along with soda solution, into batter.

With large spoon pour several buckwheat cakes onto hot griddle and bake until bubbles begin to break. Turn once and bake on other side until cakes are brown around edges.

Serve immediately with butter, syrup, molasses, honey, applesauce, or jelly.


## BUTTERMILK PANCAKES FOR TWO

*Makes 9–12 pancakes.* These are so easy to eat that if the cook's not careful he or she may not get a fair share!

| | |
|---|---|
| ¾ | cup sifted unbleached white flour |
| 2 | Tbsp wheat germ |
| 1 | tsp baking powder |
| ½ | tsp baking soda |
| 1 | tsp salt |
| 1 | egg |
| ½ | cup buttermilk |
| ½ | cup sweet milk |
| 1 | Tbsp dairy sour cream |
| 3 | Tbsp melted butter |

Put griddle over low heat.

In medium-size bowl mix ¾ cup white flour, 2 Tbsp wheat

germ, 1 tsp baking powder, ½ tsp baking soda, and 1 tsp salt.

In separate bowl or measuring cup, combine 1 egg, ½ cup buttermilk, ½ cup sweet milk, 1 Tbsp dairy sour cream, and 3 Tbsp melted butter and beat together.

Pour liquid ingredients into dry ingredients and beat until smooth.

Lightly grease griddle. With large spoon or ladle pour out batter onto griddle to make pancakes your favorite size. When tops of pancakes have risen and show bubbles all over, turn over and cook until edges are brown.

Serve hot with applesauce, honey, molasses, or maple syrup.

## BANANA WHOLE WHEAT PANCAKES

*Makes about 24 pancakes.* Delicious and exotic-tasting with the delightful flavor of banana. This recipe originated in Africa, where adults have difficulty digesting milk. Therefore, there isn't any in this recipe!

| | |
|---|---|
| 1 | cup whole wheat flour |
| 2 | tsp baking powder |
| 1 | tsp salt |
| 2 | eggs, slightly beaten |
| 2 | Tbsp melted butter |
| ¼ | cup light brown sugar |
| ¼ | tsp ground cloves, cinnamon, or allspice |
| 4 | overripe, very soft bananas |
| 1 | Tbsp lemon or lime juice |

Preheat griddle.

In medium-size bowl mix together 1 cup whole wheat flour, 2 tsp baking powder, and 1 tsp salt. (You can add a little wheat germ, if you like.) In separate container beat together 2 eggs,

2 Tbsp melted butter, ¼ cup light brown sugar with the lumps broken up, and ¼ tsp ground cloves, cinnamon, or allspice.

Pour liquid ingredients into dry. Beat batter until smooth.

Mash or liquefy bananas and add 1 Tbsp lemon or lime juice. Add to batter and beat until smooth.

Lightly grease preheated griddle with butter. Drop batter by tablespoon or ladle on griddle and bake until bubbles form. Turn over and bake on other side.

Very nice plain, with butter, sour cream, or honey.

## SOUR CREAM OATMEAL PANCAKES

*Makes about 12 3½-inch to 4-inch pancakes.* These have a very good texture and are delicious served with maple syrup, molasses, or honey. They are not as good served with fruit as other pancakes.

| | |
|---|---|
| 2 | eggs |
| ¾ | cup sour cream |
| ¼ | cup milk |
| ¼ | cup oat flour or whole wheat flour |
| ¼ | cup wheat germ |
| ¼ | cup unsifted unbleached white flour |
| ¼ | cup rolled oats |
| ½ | tsp baking soda |
| ¼ | tsp salt |

Preheat griddle while preparing batter.

Place 2 eggs, ¾ cup sour cream, and ¼ cup milk in medium-size bowl or blender and beat or blend until mixed. Add ¼ cup oat flour or whole wheat flour, ¼ cup wheat germ, ¼ cup white flour, ¼ cup rolled oats, ½ tsp baking soda, and ¼ tsp salt. Either beat until well blended and smooth or blend in blender.

Using large spoon or ¼-cup measure, pour enough batter on ungreased griddle to make 3½-inch to 4-inch pancakes. Turn

---

when bubbles form on top and brown other side. Serve immediately.

## RYE FLOUR PANCAKES

*Makes about 20 6-inch pancakes.* Here's an unusual and delicious taste treat which has to be tried. Best served with syrup, honey, or molasses. This recipe is adapted from a wheat-free one in *El Molino Best Recipes.*

> 3 eggs, separated
> 1½ cups milk
> ½ tsp salt
> 2 Tbsp honey
> 3 Tbsp melted butter
> 1½ cups rye flour

Preheat pancake griddle.

In large mixing bowl beat vigorously 3 egg yolks. Add 1½ cups milk, ½ tsp salt, 2 Tbsp honey, and 3 Tbsp melted butter, beating all the while. Beat in 1½ cups rye flour until smooth.

In a separate container whip 3 egg whites until stiff and fold into batter.

Pour batter from large spoon or ladle onto preheated ungreased griddle in pools. Bake until bubbles appear and then turn over and bake on other side.

# ALICE'S OLD-FASHIONED POTATO PANCAKES

*Makes about 14 pancakes.* The taste is accented by the onion.

         6    medium-size or 2 pounds potatoes
              Medium-size onion, minced or grated
         3    Tbsp unsifted unbleached white flour
         2    eggs, slightly beaten
         2    tsp salt
        1/8   tsp pepper
        1/2   tsp grated nutmeg
         2    Tbsp minced fresh parsley
                  or 1 Tbsp dried parsley
       3–4    Tbsp butter

If using heavy griddle put on to heat at low temperature. If using large frying pan, wait until batter is ready before heating pan.

Wash and peel potatoes. Cover with cool water. Coarsely grate potatoes and drain off excess water which may collect. (Cut potatoes finer after grating, if you prefer.) Add 1 minced medium-size onion and mix. Add 3 Tbsp white flour, 2 slightly beaten eggs, 2 tsp salt, 1/8 tsp pepper, 1/2 tsp grated nutmeg, and 2 Tbsp minced fresh parsley or 1 Tbsp dried parsley. Mix thoroughly. (Potato mixture will be very coarse and not like a pancake batter.)

Butter preheated griddle or large frying pan and place large spoonfuls of potato mixture on griddle or in hot pan. Flatten with spatula. Bake until brown and crisp on each side. Serve hot with sour cream, stewed apples, applesauce, or your favorite fruit.

If you have more than enough, continue baking pancakes but not as brown. Remove from pan, cool, and store, covered, in refrigerator. When ready to use, place pan or griddle over very low heat, butter it, and put in pancakes. Bake until brown and hot.

# CAROL'S BLENDER POTATO PANCAKES

*Makes about 12 small pancakes.* Delicious and just enough for two.

> 2   eggs
> 1   medium onion, chopped
> 1   tsp salt
> ¼   cup unsifted unbleached white flour
> ¼   tsp baking powder
> 2   cups cubed raw potatoes

Put griddle over low heat.

In blender put 2 eggs, 1 chopped onion, 1 tsp salt, ¼ cup white flour, ¼ tsp baking powder, and 2 cups cubed raw potatoes.

Cover blender and set at low speed until potatoes are grated. Be careful not to overblend. Pour batter onto preheated and lightly greased griddle to make 3-inch to 4-inch pancakes. Press down with spatula.

When bubbles start to appear and pancakes have browned, turn over with spatula and brown on other side.

Serve hot with applesauce and cinnamon and sugar, sour cream, or your favorite jam.

# WEST SIDE JOHNNY CAKES

*Makes 12 cakes.* Very rich, full corn flavor, a particular favorite with Southerners.

> 1   egg
> 1½   cups milk
> 1   tsp salt
> 1½   cups cornmeal

Put griddle over low heat. Grease lightly with corn oil or butter.

---

Beat together 1 egg and 1½ cups milk. Add 1 tsp salt and 1½ cups cornmeal. Stir until smooth. (Keep stirring from time to time while making Johnny Cakes.)

Pour 3-inch pools of batter onto heated griddle. Bake until edges are dry and begin to brown, then turn and bake other side.

Serve hot with butter and molasses or syrup.


## PEKING DOILIES

*Makes 10 doilies.* Light and crunchy.

| | |
|---|---|
| 2¼ | cups unsifted unbleached white flour |
| ½ | cup brown rice flour |
| ½ | tsp salt |
| 1 | cup boiling water |
| ¼–½ | cup peanut oil (plus extra oil for rolling) |

In large bowl mix 2 cups white flour with ½ cup brown rice flour, ½ tsp salt, and 1 cup boiling water. Knead for 2–3 minutes, adding more flour as necessary for smooth, slightly sticky dough. Divide dough into 10 equal parts. Form dough into balls. Cut each ball in half through center.

On lightly floured board, roll out each ½ ball to make circle about 5 inches in diameter. These should be thin but not so thin that they tear. Rub one side of each circle with oil.

Stack 2 circles together, oiled side to oiled side. Sprinkle some flour lightly on outsides. Roll new circles to pancake size, about 7–8 inches in diameter.

Pour ¼–½ cup peanut oil into small frying pan. Test it for heat by dropping in tiny piece of dough. When it comes to surface quickly, oil is ready. (Remember not to let oil smoke.) Fry doilies one at a time until light brown and crisp on one side. Flip over with spatula and fry same way on other side. Drain doily well on paper towels and keep warm in oven while preparing others. Serve warm.

# Waffles

# WAFFLE IRON PREPARATION

If properly tempered in the beginning when new, most waffle irons needn't and shouldn't be greased each time before use.

To temper a waffle iron, brush lightly with cooking oil before the first use. Turn it on, set the control on dark or hot, pour the batter in, and bake until done. Take this first waffle out and throw it away as it will be saturated with oil. Proceed with making waffles, but first turn control down to medium or medium-hot.

Before cleaning, allow iron to cool. Take damp cloth and mild soap and go over the outside surface. If necessary, wipe grids inside with damp cloth or paper towel too.

If there is sufficient butter in the batter itself, and the iron is not too hot, the waffle will not stick. If it does, add a little more butter, 1 tablespoon at a time—to the batter, not the iron!

# WAFFLE IRON TEMPERATURE

If waffle iron has a heat regulator or control, set it at medium-hot.

If temperature or heat control is lacking or not working, don't panic. Here's a test to determine whether or not iron is ready: Sprinkle grids with drops of water. If water jumps around before evaporating, iron is hot enough. However, if water sizzles and vaporizes immediately, take the time to let the iron cool before testing again and baking the waffles.

# BAKING

Bake waffles until steam stops coming from edges of iron, color is to your satisfaction, and iron opens easily. With fork carefully lift off waffle and serve.

# RICH WAFFLES

*Makes about 7 or 8 small round waffles or 3 very large waffles.*
Delicious served with syrup, honey, or with fresh applesauce
and cinnamon and sugar, which is the way Diana used to eat
them at home.

| | |
|---|---|
| 9 | Tbsp melted butter |
| 1¾ | cups sifted unbleached white flour |
| 3 | tsp baking powder |
| 1 | tsp salt |
| 3 | eggs, separated |
| 1¼ | cups milk |

Heat waffle iron while preparing batter.

Melt 9 Tbsp butter and set aside.

Sift together in large bowl 1¾ cups flour, 3 tsp baking
powder, and 1 tsp salt; mix well. Separate yolks and whites of
3 eggs, adding yolks to well in flour mixture.

With wooden spoon break yolks in well. Gradually add 1¼
cups milk, and blend egg yolks, milk, and flour mixture together. Add slightly cooled melted butter. Mix well.

Whip egg whites until stiff. When waffle iron is ready and
you are ready to start, fold stiff egg whites into batter, which
will be fairly thick and creamy.

---

*Quick Breads*

Pour batter into center of waffle iron from measuring cup, pitcher, or ladle, which we prefer. Spread batter almost to edges and bake.

## BUTTERMILK WAFFLES

*Makes about 8 small round waffles or 2½–3 large waffles.* Deliciously light and crunchy.

|        |                                    |
|--------|------------------------------------|
| 6–7    | Tbsp melted butter                 |
| 1½     | cups sifted unbleached white flour |
| 2      | tsp baking powder                  |
| 1      | tsp baking soda                    |
| 1      | tsp salt                           |
| ¼      | cup soy flour                      |
| 2      | Tbsp wheat germ                    |
| 2      | eggs, separated                    |
| 1½–1¾  | cups buttermilk                    |

Preheat waffle iron while preparing batter.

Melt 6–7 Tbsp butter and set aside.

Sift together 1½ cups white flour, 2 tsp baking powder, 1 tsp baking soda, and 1 tsp salt. Add ¼ cup soy flour and 2 Tbsp wheat germ and mix.

Separate yolks and whites of 2 eggs. Drop egg yolks in well in flour mixture. Gradually add 1½ cups buttermilk and beat mixture with wooden spoon until smooth. Add melted butter and blend into batter.

Whip egg whites with rotary beater until stiff and gently fold into batter just before pouring into waffle iron. (If batter is too thick add additional ¼ cup buttermilk 1 tablespoon at a time, blending all the while.)

Using measuring cup, small pitcher, or ladle, pour batter into center of waffle iron. Spread batter almost to edges. Close and bake.

# WHOLE WHEAT WAFFLES

*Makes about 7 or 8 round waffles or 3 large square waffles.*
They have a nutty whole wheat flavor—enjoy them with honey,
syrup or your favorite concoction of fruits or nuts.

|          |                           |
|----------|---------------------------|
| About ½  | cup melted butter         |
| 1⅔       | cups whole wheat flour    |
| 4        | tsp baking powder         |
| 1        | tsp salt                  |
| 2        | eggs, separated           |
| 1½       | cups milk                 |
| 1–2      | Tbsp honey                |

Preheat waffle iron while preparing batter.

Melt ½ cup butter. Set aside.

Sift together 1⅔ cups whole wheat flour (really good with
whole wheat pastry flour), 4 tsp baking powder, and 1 tsp salt
into medium-size bowl. Lightly beat 2 egg yolks and pour into
well in flour mixture. Add up to 1½ cups milk to gain right
consistency, beating with wooden spoon. Add 1–2 Tbsp honey
and 7 Tbsp melted butter slightly cooled. (Add more butter to
batter 1 tablespoon at a time if first waffle sticks.) Blend well.

Whip 2 egg whites until stiff and gently fold into batter.

With pitcher, measuring cup, large spoon or ladle, pour about
½ cup batter onto waffle iron, spreading almost to edges. Bake
and serve.

# PECAN OR WALNUT WAFFLES

Follow directions for any of basic waffle recipes. Sprinkle a
handful of coarsely chopped nuts over batter as soon as you
pour it into iron. The amount of nuts will depend on individual
preference and size of waffle iron. We always like to use a lot.
Bake immediately.

# BLUEBERRY WAFFLES

Follow directions for any of basic waffle recipes. Naturally fresh berries are best but if using canned or frozen, drain them well. Depending on size of iron, sprinkle about ¼–½ cup berries over each waffle as soon as you pour batter into iron. Remember that addition of berries makes waffle much more delicate to handle. Bake and enjoy.

# BELGIAN WAFFLES MADE WITH YEAST

*Makes 7 round waffles about 11½ inches in diameter.* In Belgium this batter is usually baked in special deep irons not generally available here. Baking them on your own iron, you will find that they are a little softer in texture than other waffles. Delicious served with whipped cream or sour cream and strawberries, blackberries, or your favorite fruit.

|         |                                      |
|---------|--------------------------------------|
| ¼       | cup melted butter                    |
| 1       | Tbsp or pkg dry yeast                |
| ½       | cup water, body temperature          |
| 1       | Tbsp wheat germ                      |
| 1       | Tbsp soy flour                       |
| About 2 | cups sifted unbleached white flour   |
| ¼       | cup light brown sugar                |
| ¼       | tsp salt                             |
| 2       | eggs, separated                      |
| 1       | cup milk, room temperature           |
| ½       | tsp vanilla flavoring                |

In saucepan melt ¼ cup butter. Set aside to cool to tepid.

Sprinkle 1 Tbsp yeast into ½ cup water, body temperature, and stir. Set aside until foamy.

In bottom of 2-cup measure put 1 Tbsp wheat germ, sift in 1 Tbsp soy flour, and enough white flour to measure 2 cups.

---

Pour flour into large bowl. Add ¼ cup light brown sugar with lumps broken up, and ¼ tsp salt. Mix.

Separate 2 eggs. Drop egg yolks into well in flour mixture, add 1 cup milk, room temperature, and yeast mixture. Beat. (A wire whisk is good to use, as lumps quickly disappear.) Add ¼ cup melted butter and ½ tsp vanilla. Beat again.

Whip egg whites with rotary beater until stiff. Gently fold into batter. Let batter stand for 1 hour or longer, stirring it about every 15 minutes. Bake in preheated waffle iron.

## BEER WAFFLES

*Makes about 8 waffles 7½ inches round.* These waffles are really different because the beer makes them nice and crisp on the outside while they remain soft on the inside. They also give off a delectable aroma of beer and lime or lemon.

| | |
|---|---|
| 4 | cups sifted unbleached white flour |
| ½ | tsp salt |
| 2 | Tbsp grated lemon or lime peel |
| 1 | Tbsp fresh lemon or lime juice |
| ⅓ | cup melted butter |
| 2 | eggs, separated |
| 3 | cups or 2 12-ounce cans light beer, room temperature |

In deep bowl combine 4 cups white flour, ½ tsp salt, and 2 Tbsp grated lemon or lime peel. Stir. Add 1 Tbsp lemon or lime juice and ⅓ cup melted butter. Separate 2 eggs and place egg yolks in deep bowl with dry ingredients. In small container whip egg whites until stiff. Set aside.

Stir and beat flour mixture, adding beer about 1 cup at a time. When batter is light, very liquid, and smooth, fold in stiffly beaten egg whites.

Let batter stand at room temperature for 1 hour. Stir from time to time and bake in preheated waffle iron.

These waffles are best served with whipped cream, jam, fruit, or sugar. They are not very good with syrup.

# Unleavened Breads
# and Crackers

# THIN AND CRUNCHY

Unleavened breads come up in almost every culture and continent—in America, India, Mexico, China, Israel, Pakistan, Afghanistan, Greece, etc.

As these breads and crackers require little or no rising time, they can be made up with no advance planning (as long as you've got the correct ingredients stockpiled), and can be munched practically straight from the oven or frying pan (the longer they cool, the crunchier, however).

Crackers can be made from the excess dough of most bread batches by adding a little extra flour to stiffen the dough, rolling it out about ⅛ inch thick with a rolling pin, and cutting it with a glass or cookie cutter. Then preheat your oven to 350° and bake until brown, about 10–20 minutes, turning if necessary.

# AMERICAN INDIAN BREAD

*Makes about 12 pieces of bread.* Here is a North American unleavened bread recipe which puffs when you fry it.

    1½   cups unsifted unbleached white flour
    1½   cups corn flour
    1   tsp salt
    1   cup water, body temperature
       Peanut oil

In medium-size bowl combine 1½ cups white flour, 1½ cups corn flour, and 1 tsp salt. Mix in 1 cup water, body temperature. Knead dough until smooth (about 5 minutes).

Separate dough into 11 or 12 small pieces. Cover these pieces with a towel and let them stand for 20 minutes.

On lightly floured board, roll each piece out thin. Heat 1 inch peanut oil in pot or deep frying pan and test it for readiness by dropping in tiny piece of dough. If it comes to surface quickly, oil is ready.

Fry each piece in oil until golden brown on both sides. Pieces should puff up well when placed in oil. Drain them on paper towels. Serve warm or cold.

# CHAPATIES OR ROTIS

*Makes about 12 flat chapaties.* The chapati is a very popular Indian bread which tastes particularly delicious with such things as curries and yogurt.

    1   cup unsifted unbleached white flour
    1   cup whole wheat flour
    ½   tsp salt

          2    Tbsp peanut oil (plus a little extra
                 for greasing your board)
      ½–¾    cup water

In a large bowl, combine 1 cup white flour, 1 cup whole
wheat flour, and ½ tsp salt. Thoroughly mix in 2 Tbsp oil. Add
½ cup water. If dough breaks up, add more water so that it
holds together and is slightly sticky.

Grease board with a little oil. Knead dough on this until
smooth (about 10 minutes). The more you knead, the lighter
chapaties will be. Make dough into ball. Break it into 12 parts.
(Try to keep dough rather moist until ready for use; otherwise
chapaties will not puff up.) Make 12 balls and press each flat
by hand. Flour your board and roll each ball out to about 6
inches in diameter and about ¹⁄₁₆ inch thick.

Heat greaseless frying pan. Place 1 chapati in pan and leave
it for ½ minute. Turn it over and leave it another ½ minute,
moving bread constantly with your fingers or shaking pan back
and forth to keep it from sticking. Each side should have
brown spots on it. If you leave your chapaties out for a time,
reheat them in dry or greaseless frying pan.

Diana's Indian friend, Raj Gupta, told her how to make
chapaties puff up. After drying them in greaseless pan, pick
them up with a pair of tongs and hold them over direct heat
such as flame or your electric heating element until they puff
up and are done. Eat them as soon as possible with or without
butter.

---

# PARATHAS

*Makes about 8 parathas.* These are flat Indian breads which can also be stuffed. They are then considered a gourmet treat. Since parathas are very bland, they are excellent to serve with spicy Eastern dishes. Recipe can be made with all whole wheat flour.

| | |
|---:|:---|
| ½ | cup unsifted unbleached white flour |
| 1¼ | cups whole wheat flour |
| ½ | tsp salt |
| 3 | Tbsp butter |
| About ⅓–½ | cup water |
| About ½ | cup melted butter |

Combine in medium-size bowl ½ cup white flour, 1¼ cups whole wheat flour, and ½ tsp salt. Rub in 3 Tbsp butter. Add enough water to make soft, moist dough. Cover with damp towel and let stand for about 1 hour. (This gives flour chance to absorb more of moisture but is not essential.)

Pull off piece of dough about 1 inch in diameter and roll into ball. Flatten ball and roll out into circle about ¹⁄₁₆ inch thick, keeping its shape as nearly round as possible. Brush with melted butter, sprinkle on a little flour to absorb butter, roll up jelly roll fashion, and then form snail-shaped ball, tucking end underneath. Roll ball out again in circle, spread with melted butter, sprinkle on a little flour, roll up, and form snail-shaped ball. Continue this process as many times as you like and have time for. (Diana's friend Raj Gupta claims that his grandmother used to build up to 8 layers of butter.) Repeat with remaining pieces of dough.

Finally, roll out each ball very thin and fry each paratha in a heavy skillet brushed with butter. Fry on both sides until crisp and brown, adding more butter as necessary. Serve immediately, keep warm in low oven, or store in refrigerator and heat up again in oven.

# INDIAN PURIS

*Makes about 12 puris.* These flat breads are very nice with curry and spicy food.

|        |                       |
|-------:|-----------------------|
| 3      | cups whole wheat flour |
| 1      | tsp salt              |
| 3      | Tbsp peanut oil       |
| More than 1 | cup water         |
|        | Additional oil for frying |

In large bowl combine 3 cups whole wheat flour, 1 tsp salt, and 3 Tbsp peanut oil. Slowly add a little more than 1 cup water, drop by drop, kneading dough until you've got slightly stiff consistency. Turn it out onto board and knead until dough becomes smooth and elastic (about 8–9 minutes). Gather into ball and place in bowl, covered with damp towel. Let dough rest about 30 minutes. (Dough can stand at room temperature longer if well covered and towel is dampened from time to time to prevent dough from drying out.)

Break off small pieces of dough and roll them into 1-inch balls.

On a lightly floured board, roll balls with small rolling pin into thin circles about $\frac{1}{16}$–$\frac{1}{8}$ inch thick. Try your best to make circles well shaped, as this will affect your puris.

In pot or deep frying pan, heat 1 inch oil. You can test it with a tiny piece of flat dough. If dough rises to surface quickly, oil is ready. With spatula, place puri in oil. (According to Raj, if you leave spatula on puri a few seconds, it will puff up more quickly.) It should rise to surface and puff up like blowfish. Fry until light brown, turn over and fry other side until light brown. Drain puris well on paper towels.

*Note:* The secret of success with Indian breads is to keep dough moist and a little sticky. As you form your puris, either fry them right away or cover them with damp towel until you are ready.

---

# SALT AND WATER CORN BREAD

J. R. Collier of Waco, Texas, ate this bread for breakfast, dinner, and supper and lived 97 years. He had local field corn ground in local mills, greatly preferring white corn. Here is how his son, Hosea Collier, writes that his wife, Lois, makes it:

"You take two cups of sifted corn meal, add one teaspoon full of salt (and if you like it, put in a little sugar, about one teaspoon full). To this gradually stir in one cup of boiling water. Stir until well mixed, then pat into a roll or into two pones. Best to form the pones with your hands. Place into greased baking pan and bake until well done. You need a hot oven, about 450°.

"Good with turnip greens or any green vegetable."


# FLOUR TORTILLAS

*Makes 12 tortillas.* Good with butter, folded into tacos, or rolled into enchiladas.

> 4   cups sifted unbleached white flour
> 2   tsp salt
> ½   cup solid vegetable shortening
> 1   cup lukewarm water

In large bowl sift 4 cups white flour and 2 tsp salt. With fingers mix in ½ cup solid vegetable shortening and 1 cup lukewarm water.

Turn dough out onto lightly floured board and knead and fold about 50 times.

Roll dough with your hands, forming long rope. Divide rope into 12 equal parts with sharp knife. Form each part into ball. Place balls on plate. Cover. Let rest 15 minutes.

---

On lightly floured board, roll each ball into flat tortilla with rolling pin. Each should be approximately 8 inches in diameter.

Heat greaseless heavy pan or skillet until drop of water dances on it.

Bake each tortilla until brown spots form on both sides. Turn only once.

## OLD CALIFORNIA
## UNLEAVENED CRACKERS

*Makes about 32 crackers.*

|       |                              |
|-------|------------------------------|
| 2     | cups sifted whole wheat flour |
| 1     | Tbsp dark brown sugar         |
| 1/2   | tsp salt                      |
| 1/4   | tsp paprika                   |
| 3/4   | Tbsp firm butter              |
| 3/4   | cup milk                      |

Preheat oven to 350°.

In large bowl mix 2 cups sifted whole wheat flour, 1 Tbsp dark brown sugar with lumps broken up, 1/2 tsp salt, and 1/4 tsp paprika.

With 2 knives or pastry blender cut in 3/4 Tbsp firm butter so that flour mixture turns into little chunks. Add 3/4 cup milk and form stiff dough.

Let dough rest for 30 minutes.

Place dough on lightly floured board. Roll it out with rolling pin about 1/8 inch thick. Cut out circles with cookie cutter or glass with 2-inch-diameter opening; or use sharp knife and cut out squares. Gather together leftover dough. Pat out and cut. Place on greased baking sheet.

Bake in preheated 350° oven for 15 minutes or until middle of crackers is baked. Cool on baking sheet.

# POPPY SEED CRACKERS

*Makes about 25 to 30 crackers.*

| | |
|---|---|
| 1 | cup sifted unbleached white flour |
| ¼ | cup cornmeal |
| 1 | tsp baking powder |
| ¼ | tsp salt |
| ¼ | tsp garlic powder |
| 1 | tsp poppy seeds |
| ½ | cup firm butter |
| 4 | Tbsp milk |

Preheat oven to 375°.

Into large bowl sift 1 cup white flour, ¼ cup cornmeal, 1 tsp baking powder, ¼ tsp salt, and ¼ tsp garlic powder. Mix in 1 tsp poppy seeds.

With 2 knives or pastry blender cut in ½ cup firm butter until mixture turns into little chunks. Mix in 4 Tbsp milk, stirring and kneading until stiff dough forms.

Turn dough out onto lightly floured board. With rolling pin, roll dough out about ⅛ inch thick. With cookie cutter, small glass, or sharp knife cut out crackers. Gather leftover dough together. Pat out and cut. Place on greased baking sheet.

Bake in preheated 375° oven for 5 minutes or until brown on bottom. Turn over with spatula and bake about another 5 minutes until brown on underside. Let cool.

# CHEDDAR CHEESE CRACKERS

*Makes 15–20 crackers.* This is what boxed commercial cheese crackers wish they were.

| | |
|---|---|
| ⅔ | cup unsifted unbleached white flour |
| ⅔ | cup grated sharp cheddar cheese |

1/4     tsp salt
1/2     tsp paprika
1     Tbsp roasted sesame seeds
3     Tbsp butter

In bowl, mix 2/3 cup white flour, 2/3 cup grated sharp cheddar cheese, 1/4 tsp salt, 1/2 tsp paprika, and 1 Tbsp roasted sesame seeds. With a pastry blender, fingertips, or 2 knives, cut in 3 Tbsp butter and mix well. Consistency of mixture should now be like coarse meal.

Knead dough on lightly floured board and form into ball.

Chill dough in refrigerator 30 minutes.

Preheat oven to 350°.

Turn dough onto lightly floured board and roll it out 1/4 inch thick with rolling pin. Cut out crackers with a knife, glass, cookie cutter, or biscuit cutter. Gather leftover dough together. Pat out and cut. Place crackers on greased baking sheet. Bake 15 minutes. Remove from oven and cool.


## CARAWAY RYE CRACKERS

*Makes about 25 crackers.*

1/4     cup soy flour
1/4     cup whole wheat flour
1     cup rye flour
1/4     cup wheat germ
2     Tbsp dark brown sugar
1/4     cup nonfat dry milk
1/2     tsp salt
1     tsp baking powder
2     Tbsp caraway seeds
1/2     cup firm butter
1     Tbsp milk

Preheat oven to 350°.

In large bowl, combine ¼ cup soy flour, ¼ cup whole wheat flour, 1 cup rye flour, ¼ cup wheat germ, 2 Tbsp dark brown sugar with lumps broken up, ¼ cup nonfat dry milk, ½ tsp salt, 1 tsp baking powder, and 2 Tbsp caraway seeds. Blend well. With pastry blender, fingertips, or 2 knives cut ½ cup firm butter into dry ingredients. When butter is well blended, mix in 1 Tbsp milk.

Turn this mixture onto floured board and knead until you get fairly stiff dough.

With rolling pin, roll dough out about ¼ inch thick. Dough may stick to pin but persevere.

Cut out crackers with knife, glass, cookie or biscuit cutter. Gather together leftover dough. Pat out and cut.

Prick each cracker with a fork. Place crackers on a greased baking sheet and bake 10 minutes. Turn crackers over and bake 5 minutes more. Remove from oven and cool.

# *Creating Your Own Recipes*

By now you have tried a number of our recipes and are ready to create a few of your own. Once you've got the basic principles in hand you can experiment freely and be pretty confident that the concoctions you create will work. Some you'll like better than others; but all will bake like, look like, feel like, and *be* bread. And the possibilities for new combinations, new taste experiences, are almost unlimited.

What follows here is a checklist of basic bread lore. Most of it summarizes information and hints given earlier in this book. Experience may well have taught you the rest.

## PROPORTION OF LIQUID AND DRY INGREDIENTS

Bread is a mixture of liquid and dry ingredients, so the proportion of one to the other is of the highest importance in bread baking. The list below gives an approximate idea of proportions in different types of bread.

*Pancakes, Waffles, and Popovers* require a liquid batter—about 1 cup dry ingredients to 1 cup liquid.

*Batter Breads, Cake-like Breads, Muffins, and Drop Biscuits* require a stiff batter or soft, sticky dough—about 2 cups dry ingredients to 1 cup liquid.

*French and Italian Bread, American Sourdough Bread, Pizza Dough, Middle Eastern Pocket Bread, and English Muffins* require a kneadable, slightly sticky dough—about $2\frac{1}{4}$–$2\frac{1}{2}$ cups dry ingredients to 1 cup liquid.

*Sour Rye, Pumpernickel, other free-standing breads, Biscuits, Scones, Flat Breads, and Crackers* require a stiff dough—about 3 cups or more dry ingredients to 1 cup liquid.

# INGREDIENT HINTS

Yeast Breads

To ensure good rising of a loaf that will hold its shape well through the final rising and baking, at least ½ of your yeast bread's flour mixture should be white or whole wheat flour. One tablespoon or 1 package dry yeast is enough for 1–3 loaves of this kind of bread.

In whole grain yeast breads use 2–3 tablespoons or packages dry yeast for 1–3 loaves of bread.

In each case 3–4 cups flour will make 1 average loaf; 6–8 cups will make 2–3 loaves.

Leavening

Too much baking powder makes a bread fall. Too little will not give enough rise. One teaspoon baking powder to 1 cup white flour or 1½ teaspoons baking powder to 1 cup heavier flours will give good results.

When using baking soda with buttermilk, molasses, or fruit juice as a leavening, the proportion (tsp/cup) should be 1:2—like ¼ teaspoon baking soda to ½ cup buttermilk, molasses, or fruit juice; or ½ teaspoon baking soda to 1 cup buttermilk, molasses, or fruit juice.

Salt

Unless you are making a salt-free bread, add 1 teaspoon salt for 3 cups flour in yeast breads. One teaspoon salt for 2 cups flour in baking powder breads.

Nuts, Fruits, Seeds

When adding these to breads, mix them well with the dry ingredients before adding the liquid ingredients.

Fat

Firm butter is essential to such recipes as Irish Soda Bread, Biscuits, Muffins, and Scones. It should be cut in with a pastry blender, knives, or fingertips and should form a mixture with the consistency of coarse crumbs. Other breads require softened or liquid fats like soft or melted butter, oil, or softened solid vegetable shortening.

In yeast breads, too much fat may prevent adequate rising. One or 2 tablespoons fat to 3–4 cups flour is usually enough. Waffles require lots and lots of butter—about $\frac{1}{4}$ cup melted butter to 1 cup flour—to keep them from sticking to the waffle iron.

## MIXING INGREDIENTS

Before mixing your liquid and dry ingredients for your own invention, study a recipe similar to the one you're doing to see how much mixing is appropriate. For instance, some yeast breads require a great deal of kneading while certain baking powder breads should be mixed as little as possible.

## RISING

Baking powder breads generally require no rising time, as they rise in the oven. Yeast breads should rise anywhere from 1 to 3 times—punching down in between. Depending upon the type of bread flour used, other ingredients, and rising temperature, your bread may take a long time to rise and double or triple in bulk. Be patient. A rising may take from 1–6 hours to overnight. Usually the first rising will take the longest.

## SHAPING

This can vary from the sublime to the ridiculous—there are the free-form shapes pancake batter makes in a hot pan; the loaf shape quick breads take on; the twisted, braided breads; the scrambled shapes of rolls. Yeast breads require one more rising after being shaped.

## BAKING

Oven Temperatures

*Yeast White Breads*—moderately hot oven, 400°
*Yeast Whole Wheat Breads*—moderate oven, 375°
*Yeast Whole Grain Breads (other than Whole Wheat)*—moderate slow oven, 350°
*Quick Breads, Biscuits, Muffins, Scones, Popovers*—quick, hot oven, 425°
*English Muffins, Pancakes, Waffles*—baked on a griddle, waffle iron, or skillet, hot enough to make a drop of water dance without evaporating.

Oven Time

Mini loaves: 30–45 minutes
Medium loaves: 45–50 minutes
Large loaves: 1 hour or more, depending on actual size and oven temperature
Biscuits and muffins: 15–35 minutes
Popovers and scones: up to 45 minutes
Pancakes and waffles: 1–5 minutes, depending on thickness.

Testing

Bake yeast breads until the outside has a good color and the bread sounds hollow when thumped with your knuckle.

Test quick breads by piercing with a cake tester, toothpick, or broom straw. If it comes out absolutely clean, your bread is done.

Pancakes, waffles, and other flat breads are done when they have begun to brown on each side.

# GLAZING AND DECORATING

If you want to glaze or coat your bread, check out our section "Glazing" for glazes made with water, butter, egg, wine, cornstarch, instant coffee, sugar, or salt water. Or invent new glazes to try, as your imagination and your own taste preferences suggest.

Decorate your bread, if you like, with seeds, salt crystals, sugar, onion, etc.

Again, don't be afraid to try new and different combinations of ingredients, shapings, final touches. Whatever the end product, it will be bread and it will be yours. We would be very interested in hearing your results. Good luck.

*Joan Wiener* and *Diana Collier*
c/o J. B. Lippincott Company
521 Fifth Avenue
New York, N. Y.   10017

# Sources of Basic
# Equipment and Ingredients

Most of the kitchen equipment you'll need for breadmaking can be found in the housewares departments of your local stores—the bread board, the pans, the sifter, etc. But some rather special tools may be easier for you to obtain by mail order (see below).

As for the ingredients you'll use, many are standard items in supermarkets. Standard Milling Company of Kansas City was one of the first to market unbleached white flour in groceries and supermarkets. Their Hecker's and Ceresota flours have been sold in stores in some parts of the country for many years, and the quality is consistently good. Currently other large companies are responding to the public demand for unbleached white flour and are marketing it through supermarkets, but we have not experimented with their products enough to be sure of their quality. You can do this, and depending on what part of the country you live in, you may also find other brands of unbleached white flour produced by smaller regional companies.

Toasted wheat germ is usually to be found among cereal products in the supermarkets; raw wheat germ, which we prefer, is a health food item.

Both of us have found that we buy many things in our local health food stores, and we strongly recommend that you try to locate one or more near you. (A few supermarkets, too, have installed special health food departments offering a limited range of products.) Health foods are natural, delicious, and convenient to use. Experiment until you find the brands that are most satisfactory to you.


The following companies will send out catalogs or price lists describing their products which range from 1- to 100-pound bags of flour to baking pans and goose-feather brushes. In picking a mail order supplier, do so by location and amounts needed. Try different companies to decide whose products you prefer, as they do differ.

Bazar Français
666 Sixth Avenue
New York, N.Y. 10010
> Complete line of imported quality cooking and baking equipment such as saucepans, pastry scrapers, rolling pins, baking pans, wire whisks, etc.

Byrd Mill Company
P.O. Box 5167
Richmond, Va. 23220
> Excellent source of high quality organic or natural stone-ground flour and cereals. 1- to 2-pound bags.

Deer Valley Farm and Country Store
R.D. 1
Guilford, N.Y. 13780
> Organically grown wheat flour, cereals, and meal available in 1-, 2-, 5-, 10-, 25-, and 100-pound bags; also yeast, nuts, soya products, dried fruits, seeds, malt extract, etc.

El Molino Mills
345 Baldwin Park Boulevard
City of Industry, Calif. 91744
> Complete line of organically grown grains, flour, cereals, seeds, yeast, etc.

Fern Soya Foods
4520 James Place
Melrose Park, Ill. 60160
> Specializing in complete line of soy products and organically grown wheat flour; primarily distributors but will sell to large-volume users (100-pound bags).

Maid of Scandinavia
3245 Raleigh Avenue
Minneapolis, Minn. 55416
> Extensive line of baking equipment including rolling pins, bread pans, measures, scales, thermometers, wire whisks, etc.

Paprikas Weiss
1546 Second Avenue
New York, N.Y. 10028

Limited but interesting selection of organic whole grain
flours and cereals stone ground; extensive line of imported
cooking and baking equipment including feather brushes,
scrapers, flour grinders, rolling pins, fresh herb starter sets,
etc.

The Sioux Millers
R.R. 1
Whiting, Ia. 51063

Freshly stone-ground flour from high quality grains—fine
and coarse; also organic whole grains, meals, cereals, seeds,
honeys, oils, syrups, teas, nuts, etc. 1-, 3-, 5-, 10-, and 25-
pound bags.

Walnut Acres, Inc.
Penns Creek, Pa. 17862

Carefully described freshly ground organic and nonorganic
grain products stored in refrigerated bins (1-, 3-, 5-, and 10-
pound bags); also seeds, teas, dried fruits, unsulphured
molasses, honeys, nuts, dried spices; various equipment such
as bread pans, grinding mills, etc.

# *Measurements*

A     pinch or dash = ⅛ tsp
3     tsp  = 1 Tbsp
2     Tbsp = 1 fluid ounce
4     Tbsp = ¼ cup
5⅓   Tbsp = ⅓ cup
8     Tbsp = ½ cup
10⅔  Tbsp = ⅔ cup
12    Tbsp = ¾ cup
⅞    cup = 1 level cup minus 2 Tbsp
16    Tbsp or 8 fluid ounces = 1 cup
2     cups = 1 pint
2     pints or 4 cups = 1 quart

*Solid fats in sticks or pounds*

1     pound = 2 cups
½    pound or 2 sticks = 1 cup
¼    pound or 1 stick = ½ cup = 8 Tbsp
½    stick = ¼ cup = 4 Tbsp

*Oven Temperatures*

slow = 275°–325°
moderate = 325°–375°
moderately hot = 375°–400°
hot = 400°–450°
very hot = 450°–500°

1 cup unsifted white flour = about 1¼ cup sifted white flour.
Whole grain flours are not sifted; white flour is always sifted before measuring unless otherwise specified. Approximations should be made only by the experienced baker.

# Index

---

| DATE | | | |
|---|---|---|---|
| OCT 2 1991 | | | |
| | | | |
| | | | |
| | | | |
| | | | |
| | | | |
| | | | |
| | | | |
| | | | |
| | | | |
| | | | |